AIR CAMPAIGN

LEGION CONDOR
1936–39

The Luftwaffe develops *Blitzkrieg* in the Spanish Civil War

T0323081

JAMES S. CORUM | ILLUSTRATED BY GRAHAM TURNER

OSPREY PUBLISHING
Bloomsbury Publishing Plc
PO Box 883, Oxford, OX1 9PL, UK
1385 Broadway, 5th Floor, New York, NY 10018, USA
E-mail: info@ospreypublishing.com
www.ospreypublishing.com

OSPREY is a trademark of Osprey Publishing Ltd

First published in Great Britain in 2020

A catalogue record for this book is available from the British Library.

ISBN: PB 9781472840073; eBook 9781472840080; ePDF 9781472840059;
XML 9781472840066

20 21 22 23 24   10 9 8 7 6 5 4 3 2 1

Maps by bounford.com
Diagrams by Adam Tooby
3D BEVs by Paul Kime
Index by Janet Andrew
Typeset by PDQ Digital Media Solutions, Bungay, UK
Printed and bound in India by Replika Press Private Ltd.

Artist's note
Readers may care to note that the original paintings from which the colour plates in this
book were prepared are available for private sale. All reproduction copyright whatsoever is
retained by the publishers. All enquiries should be addressed to:
Graham Turner, PO Box 568, Aylesbury, Bucks. HP17 8ZX UK www.studio88.co.uk
The publishers regret that they can enter into no correspondence upon this matter.

Osprey Publishing supports the Woodland Trust, the UK's leading woodland conservation
charity.

To find out more about our authors and books visit www.ospreypublishing.com. Here
you will find extracts, author interviews, details of forthcoming events and the option to
sign up for our newsletter.

Acknowledgements
The author would like to thank the von Richthofen family for their very generous access
to the family's archives, including correspondence, papers and photos.

CONTENTS

ORIGINS

From the airlift to Madrid

The trimotor Junkers Ju 52 came into service in 1932 as a civilian transport. The Ju 52 was easily modified into a bomber and, as it was already in production, it was used by the Luftwaffe as a bomber until purpose-built aircraft like the He 111 became available. The Ju 52 bomber carried the bombardier in a special pod that was lowered from the aircraft. The Ju 52 carried 1,500kg of bombs. (Author's collection)

By 1936 Spain had become divided into two nations. One of these was conservative, Catholic and Nationalist. This side included Spain's small businessmen and landowners. There were large factions arguing for the return of the monarchy and these had formed militia forces, especially in the northern province of Navarre. The 1930s had also seen the rise of a large Fascist party, the Falange, modelled on Mussolini's example in Italy. The other Spain was a coalition of forces that held the majority in the Spanish parliament. These included socialists, radical socialists, anarchists, progressives and assorted liberals who were supported strongly by the labour unions and the poor tenant farmers. Spain had a small but well-organized Communist party as well, and this faction was quickly winning adherents.

Since the defeat of an attempted right-wing coup d'état in 1932, the two Spains became ever more polarized. By summer of 1936 right-wing forces led by a coalition of army generals were deep in planning for a national uprising. The uprising itself was triggered on 13 July 1936 when Calvo Sotelo, the leader of right-wing opposition in the Spanish parliament, was arrested and then assassinated by the government police. A few days later, on 16–17 July 1936, much of the Spanish Army, backed by an assortment of monarchists, conservatives and Fascists, went into open revolt against the Republic. The Nationalist rebellion was led by a small junta of generals. General José Sanjurjo, who had led the attempted rightest coup in 1932 and was imprisoned and then amnestied by the government, lived in exile in Portugal and was the most senior of the coup plotters. Another senior officer was General Emilio Mola, a decorated veteran of the North African wars who had served as the governor-general and commandant in Pamplona, Navarre. Mola had developed excellent contacts with the large monarchist movement in northern Spain. The third senior leader of the Nationalist junta was General Francisco Franco, at 44 the youngest of the top leaders.

Franco was one of the best known and most successful generals in the Spanish Army. He had remained generally aloof from politics, and stayed away from earlier coup attempts and revolutionary activity, but had fallen under the suspicion of the Republic's government and been sent far away to the Canary Islands to serve as commander there. However, Franco was also an exceptionally capable officer and was the most highly decorated combat commander in the Spanish Army. He was a battlefield soldier known for his bravery and coolness under fire when he fought in the North African wars. He had been wounded several times and had, in turn, been the youngest captain, major, colonel and general in the Spanish Army. (He was promoted to general at age 33.) From 1923 to 1927 he had commanded the Spanish Foreign Legion during the Rif War in Morocco. When the coup began, Franco's mission was to fly on the night of 16/17 July from the Canary Islands to North Africa to raise the garrison there to support the coup. Not only was Franco well-known in North Africa, but gaining control of the Spanish Army of Africa was key to the Nationalists' hopes of taking Spain.

The Spanish Peninsular Army was, for the most part, a poorly trained force with obsolete equipment and far too many ageing officers. In 1936 it consisted of about 100,000 men. The police forces of the Spanish Republic, which included the Civil Guards and the Assault Police, were another 60,000 men. The army on the Spanish mainland and Civil Guards were split in their sympathies, with about half of these forces going to each side. However, the Nationalists had an advantage in terms of securing Army support in that the vast majority of officers were supportive of the Nationalist coup, and in the

General Francisco Franco. It was Franco who sent representatives to Germany and Italy to obtain support for the Nationalist cause. (Author's collection)

area controlled by the government many of the officers either fled or were arrested. The small air force split with about 150 of the pilots staying loyal to the government and about 100 going over to the rebels. The Navy enlisted crewmen distrusted their officers, and when the coup began they arrested and executed officers suspected of Nationalist loyalties. Some warships did fall to the Nationalists, but the Spanish Navy's most powerful units, including the battleship *Jaime I*, sided with the government.

The one really effective military force in Spain – well-trained, well-equipped, and possessing considerable combat experience – was the Army of Africa, a largely volunteer force honed by decades of hard colonial campaigns in Spanish Morocco. The Army of Africa consisted of 20,000 long-term volunteers recruited from the Moroccans and a few thousand professional soldiers of the Spanish Foreign Legion. Ten thousand troops of the Peninsular Army were also stationed in Spanish Morocco. These approximately 35,000 troops included many officers, NCOs and enlisted men who were veterans of the Rif War of the 1920s. If these forces could be won over to the coup and transported to mainland Spain, they would be far superior to any government force put in their way.

However, the plan in the first days of the coup was for the rebels to seize power in the major Spanish cities of Madrid and Barcelona. On the very first day of the coup, this was attempted by army and police units. But they were defeated when the government armed the

General der Flieger Helmuth Wilberg. Before his death in an air crash in 1941, Wilberg was one of the Luftwaffe's most experienced General Staff officers. He organized and led Special Staff W in July 1936, serving as its chief until March 1938. Thanks to Special Staff W, logistics and support for the Condor Legion were managed effectively. (Author's collection)

leftist unions and militias and forced the surrender of the rightist plotters, most of whom were then executed. Most of Spain, including the major industrial areas, remained in the hands of the Republic, as did Barcelona and the capital, Madrid. One of the coup leaders, General Mola, roused the efforts of the Nationalists in northern Spain and took over most of the north, with the exception of the Basque region and Asturias. In the south, General Queipo de Llano seized power in Seville and part of the south, including the port of Cadiz. In North Africa, the officers of the Army of Africa immediately joined the Nationalist coup and turned over command to General Franco.

After one week of essentially urban combat, the boundaries between Republican and Nationalist Spain were already set. The Nationalists were frustrated by their inability to bring this first-rate army in Morocco over to the Spanish mainland. If these 30,000 well trained, experienced troops could be brought to the mainland, they would clearly be superior to any other force available in Spain. But getting the army to the mainland over the short straits between Africa and Cadiz was an impossible task, as the Republic's navy had full control of the sea. With destroyers and the battleship *Jaime I* the Republicans quickly blockaded the straits between Morocco and Spain. Unable to move by sea, General Franco turned to the idea of an airlift to fly the Army of Africa over the straits to Seville. But the Nationalists had only a handful of operational aircraft. Franco turned to Germany and Italy for help.

Germany decides for intervention: the airlift

With the Nationalist cause faltering after the initial rising, General Franco was approached by two German businessmen residing in Spanish Morocco. Adolf Langenheim and Johannes Bernhardt were members of the Nazi Party and supporters of the Spanish Nationalist cause. They believed that, with their Nazi Party connections in Germany, they could meet with Hitler and convince him to provide aircraft and support to Franco's forces. Franco gave his blessing to the mission and Bernhardt and Langenheim flew to Berlin on 25 July in a civilian German Ju 52 passenger transport. The businessmen's claim that their party connections could get them access proved true. They met with Rudolf Hess who quickly arranged for them to meet with Hitler, who that night was attending the Wagner Festival at Bayreuth. Hitler had already been briefed on the Spanish situation by his foreign ministry and both the foreign office and the military leadership wanted to avoid Spanish involvement, but Hitler agreed to meet with the businessmen. Bernhardt and Langenheim met with Hitler on the night of 25/26 July, and convinced him that some support from Germany in the form of aircraft and supplies would be to Germany's advantage; it would tip the scales in favour of the Nationalists, who would be far more amenable to pursuing pro-German trade and foreign policies than the leftist Republic.

Hitler immediately agreed to provide aircraft and military equipment to Franco and told Hermann Göring, who was attending to Hitler in Bayreuth, to make the arrangements. Göring initially had no enthusiasm for the operation, but he could move with speed and determination

Photo taken by one of the first Condor Legion members at the start of the German intervention. The Germans admired the Moroccans for their bravery and tactical competence. These troops enabled the Nationalists to connect the two Nationalist enclaves in northern and southern Spain and to begin an advance on Madrid. (Author's collection)

when it pleased the Führer. Göring got on the phone to the Luftwaffe headquarters in Berlin and ordered the Air Staff to put together a plan to support the Spanish Nationalists immediately. The next morning, 26 July, although it was a Sunday, *Generalleutnant* Helmuth Wilberg of the Luftwaffe was ordered to form a special staff in order to organize assistance to the Spanish Nationalists. The next day ten aircraft were detached from Lufthansa and sent to Franco in North Africa to begin airlifting the Army of Africa. Italy agreed to allow transit of the planes and refuel them. Italy had also been approached by Franco and, like Hitler, Mussolini agreed to send immediate help – also in the form of aircraft and military equipment. Wilberg, a

Alexander von Scheele was a *Schlachtflieger* (close-attack pilot) in World War I. He was chosen to lead the operation because he was fluent in Spanish. (USAF Historical Research Agency)

brilliant General Staff officer and one of Germany's most experienced airmen, formed a staff from officers at Luftwaffe headquarters in Berlin. Special Staff W (W for Wilberg) was issuing plans and orders within two days and by 31 July a ship with additional German aircraft, aid and personnel were on their way from Germany to Spanish Morocco. Wilberg would remain chief of the Spanish operation until his retirement in March 1938.

The first volunteers for Spain were 85 well-trained pilots, NCOs and technical personnel (all unmarried at first) who were directed to report to Hamburg for a special mission. In Hamburg they were asked to volunteer for the special mission, to be kept highly secret, which would require that they be officially retired from the Luftwaffe and placed on reserve status. They would serve outside the country. Without knowing the exact nature of their duties (one suspects that many followed the news and understood they were going to Spain) the personnel sent by their units all volunteered. Late at night on 31 July the merchant ship *Usaramo*, loaded with 85 Luftwaffe volunteers, ten Ju 52 bombers, six Heinkel He 51 fighters, 20 anti-aircraft guns, and personnel to man both the aircraft and the guns, sailed from Hamburg for Spain. They all wore civilian clothes and any correspondence was sent to a post office box in Hamburg. The small detachment was the first of many shipments of materiel and personnel for Spain, which was at first called Operation *Magic Fire*.

The He 51 was the Luftwaffe's main fighter in 1936. It had elegant lines and looked like a fine machine, but proved inferior to the Republic's Soviet-built I-15 and I-16 fighters. It was relegated to ground-attack duties, which it performed very well. (Author's collection)

The initial German directives did not include combat operations. The He 51 fighters and the flak guns were intended for self-defence only and the additional Ju 52s were intended to arm the Spanish Nationalists. Germans would train the Spaniards to fly the aircraft. General Wilberg selected an experienced Luftwaffe officer, Major Alexander von Scheele, to command the small German detachment sent to help Franco. Von Scheele was a decorated World War I *Schlachtflieger* – a pilot for an armoured and heavily armed two-seater close support aircraft. After the war and the disbanding of the Imperial Air Service, von Scheele went to South America where he was engaged in business. In the early 1930s he returned to Germany and joined the reborn Luftwaffe, where experienced pilots and former Imperial officers were needed and welcomed. Von Scheele was selected for his complete fluency in Spanish and he arrived in Spain and took command of the mission on 6 August when the *Usaramao* docked at the port of Cadiz.

At this point it should be noted that the Nationalist junta had not formally created a state. So, the agreement the Germans and Italians had with the Nationalists was not with any provisional government, but merely a personal agreement with Franco. Although Franco was initially the junior partner in the Nationalist leadership due to his age and lower level of visibility in right-wing circles, he was catapulted to the top spot by events. General Sanjurjo, who saw himself as the senior Nationalist leader, was killed on 20 July when his plane, flying from Portugal, crashed just after take-off. General Mola controlled the key regions of northern Spain and had good connections to the monarchists and rightists in the northern provinces but did not have command of the elite Spanish Army of Africa that would be the key card of the Nationalists. It was Franco who took the initiative to seek, and win, support from Germany and Italy. And it was this support and the Army of Africa that would determine whether the Nationalist rebellion would succeed.

Upon arriving in Spain, von Scheele met with Franco and set up an arrangement to provide a legal cover for the German aid to the Nationalists. A front company, the Spanish German Transport Company Limited, operating under the Spanish acronym HISMA, was

Ju 52 carrying Spanish Moroccan troops from Tétouan to Seville, summer 1936. The airlift of the Spanish Army of Africa, along with 200m tonnes of equipment, saved the Nationalist cause in the first weeks of the Spanish Civil War. (Author's collection)

created to manage the aid and financial credits to the Nationalists. Franco, for his part, was willing to commit to providing Germany with privileged access to Spain's mineral resources, an important consideration since Germany was rearming and looking for reliable sources of raw materials.

The first Luftwaffe force to be committed to the Nationalist cause was a group of ten Ju 52 transports taken from Lufthansa, which were deployed by flying them from Germany, refuelling in Italy, and then flying them on to Spanish Morocco. Before the end of July, a full airlift was underway with German transports flying from Tétouan Airfield in Morocco to Seville, an hour's flight. Normally a passenger load for a Ju 52 was 17 passengers, but as many as 40 Moroccan soldiers were often crammed aboard the transports for the short flight. Before long the Germans were flying 1,200 troops a week from Africa to mainland Spain. By the week of 10–16 August 1936, the Luftwaffe transports were able to airlift 2,853 soldiers along with 7,985kg of equipment. During colonial conflicts the British and French

Bombing the battleship *Jaime I*, 13 August 1936

When the civil war began most of the Spanish Navy remained in Republican hands, including Spain's one operational battleship. The *Jaime I* was slow and obsolescent, carrying eight 12in guns, but it and its supporting destroyers effectively blocked all sea traffic between Nationalist-held Morocco and the Spanish mainland. Not only did the *Jaime I* control the seas, but its batteries of Vickers 1.9in and twin 25mm Hotchkiss anti-aircraft guns made it a threat to the German transports ferrying Nationalist troops and supplies from Morocco to the mainland.

Two weeks into the airlift von Scheele decided the battleship had to be neutralized. He ordered two of the Ju 52 transports to be converted into bombers to seek out and bomb the *Jaime I*. Learning that the battleship was moored at Malaga, the two hastily converted Ju 52s set out at 0400hrs on 13 August to attack. The first plane, piloted by Captain Baron von Moreau, got lost in the heavy morning cloud cover and returned to base. The second Ju 52, piloted by Captain Alfred Henke, with a Spanish naval officer as an observer, dropped down low through the clouds to 1,200ft and located the *Jaime I* at dawn anchored far out in the bay (likely moored away from the port for fear of an air attack).

Henke attacked at 1,200ft and dropped three 250kg bombs. Two struck the *Jaime I* in front of the bridge, causing massive damage and killing about 50 naval crew. The *Jaime I* was disabled and had to be towed up the coast to Cartagena and never again became operational. Captain Henke's successful attack was a major blow to the Republican Navy and was the first step in breaking the Republican blockade of the straits.

Condor Legion signallers just arrived in Seville, August or September 1936. Here the German signallers are enjoying a drink with Spanish troops. The first Germans in Spain arrived without uniforms and were ordered to avoid combat. That would soon change. (Author's collection)

had flown troops and supplies to far-flung outposts, but nothing on the scale of the Spanish airlift had ever been seen in warfare.

The airlift of the Nationalist forces to mainland Spain from 27 July to 11 October was a clear triumph. The German transports were joined by the Italians and the Nationalists also operated some transports, but the main effort and credit for the success belonged to the Germans, who had also managed the airfield operations. The airlift ended in October when the Nationalists won control of the sea lanes and could send men and material to Africa by ship. In two-and-a-half months, more than 20,000 Nationalist soldiers had been airlifted into Spain. Of this total over two-thirds, more than 13,000 troops, had been airlifted by the Luftwaffe along with a total of 270,199kg of equipment including machine guns, and more than 30 artillery pieces with their ammunition. The entire operation was carried out under arduous conditions with the loss of only one aircraft.

In the very first days of the German intervention in Spain, the German effort consisted of scarcely more than 20 Ju 52s and the initial six Heinkel He 51 fighters, which landed at Cadiz on 6 August. Major von Scheele organized the first hundred or so German personnel into small teams. Captain von Moreau was made commander of the Ju 52 transports and was responsible for the airlift aircraft and airfield operations. Another team was responsible for assembling the He 51 fighters and training the Spanish pilots. Another team was detailed to train the Spanish in the use of flak guns. An air depot and logistics centre were set up to oversee the assembly of aircraft and their maintenance. It soon became clear that the Nationalists needed more help so more German equipment and personnel began arriving through August.

The airlift of the Army of Africa allowed the unit's very talented soldier, Colonel José Yagüe, to form the Moroccan battalions into task forces in early August, and to move north from Seville along the Portuguese border, and finally to link up with General Mola's northern Nationalist enclave. On 14 August Yagüe's forces took the city of Badajoz on the Portuguese border, and not only linked up the two halves of Nationalist Spain but opened the Portuguese border to the Nationalists. As the Portuguese leader Salazar was sympathetic to the Nationalists, military equipment and supplies could now be brought in through Portugal. Franco, who had transferred his headquarters to Seville in early August, was ready to take command of the southern army and, along with Mola, move northeast to take Madrid.

The Germans enter combat

The great step in the conflict was taken in August 1936 when Major von Scheele authorized a German bomber attack on the battleship *Jaime I*. Republican naval superiority in the straits between Africa and mainland Spain was a nuisance to the Nationalists. The *Jaime I*'s anti-aircraft artillery batteries targeted the German transports flying overhead, forcing them to fly at high altitude. The *Jaime I* had bombarded and blockaded Cadiz, the one major port in southern Spain that belonged to the Nationalists. Putting the *Jaime I* out of action would be the first step in gaining Nationalist control of the sea lanes. Von Scheele ordered two of the Ju 52s to be modified as bombers with kits that had been included with the first shipment of equipment. Receiving intelligence on 12 August that the *Jaime I* was in the Bay of Malaga, von Scheele ordered a strike the next day with two converted Ju 52s, to be flown by Captain von Moreau and Captain Henke. The Ju 52 piloted by von Moreau failed to find the *Jaime I* in the low cloud, but the second Ju 52 did and its bombs hit the battleship, badly damaging it and taking it out of action. This highly successful mission helped turn the tide for the Nationalists in securing their hold in southern Spain. The Germans began flying combat missions in support of the Nationalist columns moving towards Madrid. Captain von Moreau redeemed his reputation as a

The Alcázar of Toledo as seen from a German aircraft. The Alcázar was a complex of buildings housing the Spanish Army Infantry Officers' School. A force of 1,300 Nationalist soldiers, police, and militia defended the Alcázar from July to October 1936. Condor Legion Captain Rudolf Freiherr von Moreau airdropped supplies into the courtyard of the main building. The spirited defence of the Alcázar in July and August 1936 provided considerable propaganda value for the Nationalists. Franco diverted the Nationalist Army's advance on Madrid to relieve the besieged forces at the Alcázar. (Author's collection)

navigator and pilot on 21 August when, under heavy ground fire, he was able to resupply the besieged Nationalist garrison at Toledo's Alcázar by dropping food canisters into the small courtyard of the Military School.

As soon as the airlift operations were functioning smoothly it was decided that some of the Ju 52 transports could be converted into bombers and used to support the Nationalist forces, which were then engaged in desperate fighting on their way to relieve the garrison of the Alcázar in Toledo and then advance to Madrid. In late August 1936 German airmen began flying small-scale bombing missions, usually in the form of harassment raids against enemy airfields. By September more Luftwaffe personnel had arrived and by the end of September a total of the 20 Ju 52 transport/bombers, 24 He 51 fighters and 29 He 46 reconnaissance aircraft/light bombers had arrived. Half of the He 51s were turned over to the Nationalists to form a fighter squadron. As the airlift wound down some of the Ju 52s were also turned over to the Nationalists to form a bomber squadron. The Nationalist Air Force was also receiving aircraft and training from the Italian Air Force, but training the Spanish crews on the new equipment would take some time.

The Nationalists form a state

By October 1936, the German presence in Spain had expanded to approximately 600 personnel, as Spain was seen as an ideal testing ground for the Luftwaffe's aircraft. A variety of aircraft arrived, including 20 Heinkel He 46s for reconnaissance and light bombing; two He 70s to serve as light bombers and reconnaissance aircraft; two He 60 naval seaplanes; one He 50 dive bomber and two Henschel Hs 123 dive bombers. Four 88mm guns and 28 20mm flak guns had arrived to serve as airfield protection for the German forces.

On 1 October, the political relationship of the German intervention in Spain changed when the informal Nationalist junta created a proper government and named General Francisco Franco as the Head of the Spanish State. The German intervention had worked very much in Franco's favour, because the initial support of the Germans was not to any Nationalist state, which did not exist, but came as a personal commitment to him. General Mola, who had not taken the initiative (like Franco) to send emissaries to Germany and Italy, had been manoeuvred out of the lead role in the Nationalist insurgency and would now play a subordinate role to Franco as the commander of the Army of the North. In the first weeks of the insurgency, a considerable amount of political machination went on, with General Alfredo Kindelan, a former commander of the Spanish Air Force, playing a central role in rounding up Spanish officer support for Franco as head of the Nationalist state rather than Mola. Kindelan was a staunch Nationalist who had resigned from the service in 1931 rather than serve a Republic, and saw that Franco was the best chance to restore a Spanish monarchy.

With the new Spanish state established, the Germans granted formal recognition to the Nationalists as the government of Spain and sent an ambassador. With the civil war progressing in the Nationalists' favour, the Germans were ready to increase their commitment to Franco. By the end of October, intelligence was received that the Soviet Union was sending significant aid to the Republic, and that Russian military advisors were already arriving in Spain. So, Berlin made the decision to reorganize the German force already in Spain and to increase support to the Nationalists.

Re-evaluating the mission

Colonel Walter Warlimont, not an airman but an Army General Staff officer with a reputation for strategic acumen, was sent to Spain by the Wehrmacht staff in late August to take command of the mission, and also to evaluate the strategic situation and report to Berlin. Warlimont was a good choice to send to Spain as von Scheele, while a good air unit commander, was out of his depth in dealing with strategic issues. Warlimont could count on the Wehrmacht staff to listen to his evaluation. To the relief of the German army commanders, Warlimont recommended against any large army force being sent to Spain. Committing a large military force would disrupt Germany's rearmament programme and also push Germany towards open confrontation with the other European powers, a confrontation that Hitler wanted to avoid in 1936. Warlimont argued for increasing the force that was already present to an air task force of 100-plus aircraft and 5,000 personnel. The German force in Spain would be renamed the Legion Condor. The army would contribute a small tank battalion for testing, small teams to train the Spanish officers, and specialist units. Surplus equipment would be made available for the Nationalist army. The force would not only aid the Nationalists, but also gain some valuable combat experience for the Luftwaffe and allow the Luftwaffe and Wehrmacht to test equipment– not just aircraft but radios, vehicles, munitions and tanks.

The limited commitment of the Legion Condor was one that the Luftwaffe, now expanding very rapidly, could readily support. Special Staff W under General Wilberg in Berlin had the pick of Luftwaffe personnel to call upon, since Luftwaffe units were initially told to ask their best-trained and qualified personnel to volunteer; these men were then told that they would be volunteered for an interesting mission, that their work would be secret, and that they would officially have to resign from the Luftwaffe. Their new status would be as Luftwaffe reservists and 'volunteers' for the Spanish Nationalists. There seem to have been few complaints and most Legion Condor airmen seem to have considered the Spanish War an adventure.

Units sent not only their best qualified personnel, but also made sure to send younger unmarried men. As word of the German involvement went through the Luftwaffe, career officers and NCOs also applied for service as volunteers with the Legion Condor. Officers, enlisted men and technicians commonly served for 6–12 months before being rotated back to Germany. With a highly trained and carefully selected group of Luftwaffe personnel, mostly NCOs and specialists, there were few discipline problems. Indeed, the Legion Condor constituted a unique organization within the Germany military. Upon returning from Spain, the Legion Condor veterans were normally promoted and sent to serve in units throughout the Luftwaffe.

A new commander

On 1 November Luftwaffe *Generalmajor* Hugo Sperrle arrived in Spain to take command of what would soon be a greatly enlarged force. Sperrle was soon followed by *Oberstleutnant* Wolfram Freiherr von Richthofen, who was initially slated to command the experimental aircraft squadron but, upon his arrival in Spain, was named chief of staff of the Legion Condor. The two would prove to be a highly effective leadership team. Sperrle was a pre-World War I aviator who commanded aviation for the 7th Army during World War I and served on the

Hugo Sperrle was one of Germany's most experienced air officers, having joined the Air Service as a general staff officer before World War I. Sperrle transformed the Condor Legion from an improvised intervention force into a formidable fighting corps. A genial Bavarian by nature, Sperrle had a fearsome appearance due to facial scars from a World War I air crash. Upon his return to Germany in late 1937, Sperrle initiated major changes in Luftwaffe training and tactics based on the Spanish war experience. (Author's collection)

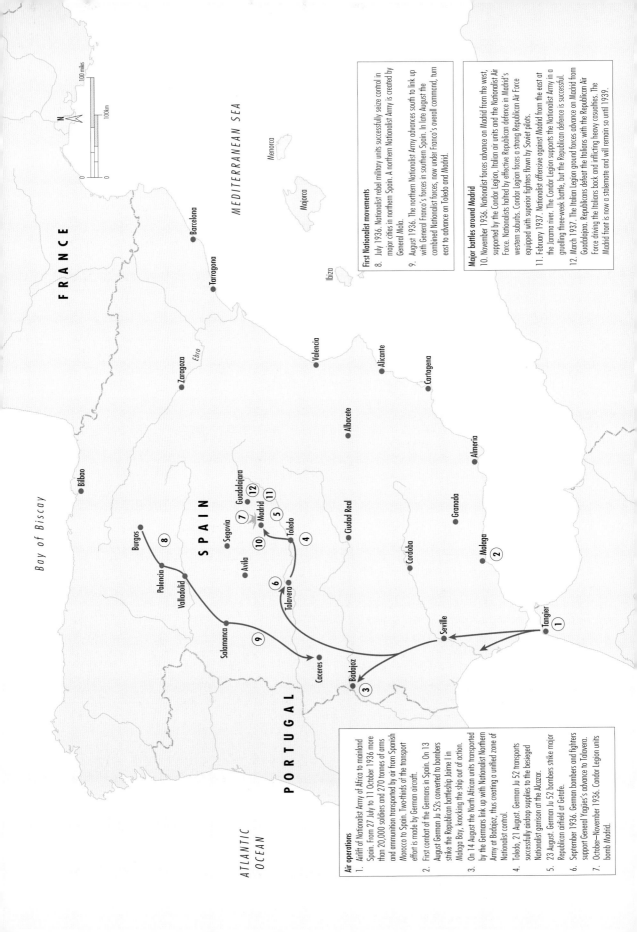

ATLANTIC OCEAN

Bay of Biscay

FRANCE

SPAIN

PORTUGAL

MEDITERRANEAN SEA

Menorca

Majorca

Ibiza

Cities and locations:
Bilbao, Burgos, Palencia, Valladolid, Salamanca, Cáceres, Badajoz, Segovia, Ávila, Talavera, Toledo, Madrid, Guadalajara, Zaragoza, Ebro, Ciudad Real, Córdoba, Granada, Málaga, Seville, Tangier, Valencia, Albacete, Alicante, Cartagena, Almería, Tarragona, Barcelona

N

0   100km
0   100 miles

Air operations

1. Airlift of Nationalist Army of Africa to mainland Spain. From 27 July to 11 October 1936 more than 20,000 soldiers and 270 tonnes of arms and ammunition transported by air from Spanish Morocco to Spain. Two-thirds of the transport effort is made by German aircraft.

2. First combat of the Germans in Spain. On 13 August German Ju 52s converted to bombers strike the Republican battleship Jaime I in Malaga Bay, knocking the ship out of action.

3. On 14 August the North African units transported by the Germans link up with Nationalist Northern Army at Badajoz, thus creating a unified zone of Nationalist control.

4. Toledo, 21 August. German Ju 52 transports successfully airdrop supplies to the besieged Nationalist garrison at the Alcazar.

5. 23 August. German Ju 52 bombers strike major Republican airfield at Getafe.

6. September 1936. German bombers and fighters support General Yagüe's advance to Talavera.

7. October–November 1936. Condor Legion units bomb Madrid.

First Nationalist movements

8. July 1936. Nationalist rebel military units successfully seize control in major cities in northern Spain. A northern Nationalist Army is created by General Mola.

9. August 1936. The northern Nationalist Army advances south to link up with General Franco's forces in southern Spain. In late August the combined Nationalist forces, now under Franco's overall command, turn east to advance on Toledo and Madrid.

Major battles around Madrid

10. November 1936. Nationalist forces advance on Madrid from the west, supported by the Condor Legion, Italian air units and the Nationalist Air Force. Nationalists halted by effective Republican defence in Madrid's western suburbs. Condor Legion forces a strong Republican Air Force equipped with superior fighters flown by Soviet pilots.

11. February 1937. Nationalist offensive against Madrid from the east at the Jarama river. The Condor Legion supports the Nationalist Army in a gruelling three-week battle, but the Republican defence is successful.

12. March 1937. The Italian Legion ground forces advance on Madrid from Guadalajara. Republicans defeat the Italians with the Republican Air Force driving the Italians back and inflicting heavy casualties. The Madrid front is now a stalemate and will remain so until 1939.

General Staff after the war. From 1927–29, Sperrle served as the Army's shadow Luftwaffe commander. He was commanding Air District V when he was called upon to serve in Spain. Sperrle was a physically imposing man, standing over 6ft tall and weighing close to 300lb. He had a fearsome appearance, mainly due to his badly scarred face – the result of a World War I aircraft crash. In fact, he had a humorous side and a reputation for enjoying good living. He was known as impatient and demanding of subordinates, but also had a reputation in the Luftwaffe's officer corps as a highly competent commander.

Generalmajor Hugo Sperrle and his chief of staff, von Richthofen, made a highly effective command team in Spain. The two of them set policies that remained in place for the whole existence of the Legion Condor. Sperrle, as senior German officer in Spain, dealt directly with Franco and his government and staff at the strategic level. Von Richthofen ran the day-to-day operations of the Legion and oversaw the operational war planning. Both Sperrle and von Richthofen were professional soldiers and neither could be said to have had a diplomatic personality.

Wolfram von Richthofen was younger than Sperrle and had served in World War I, first as a cavalry officer, and later as a fighter pilot, flying in Jagdgeschwader 1, led by his famous cousin Manfred. Like Sperrle, von Richthofen had a reputation for being a good troop leader and also tough on his subordinates. But von Richthofen had a reputation for being not just smart but brilliant. Possessing an exceptional technical mind, von Richthofen had earned an engineering degree after the world war and returned to join the Army General Staff. He then earned a PhD in engineering, with a thesis on the best means to organize mass production of heavy aircraft. From 1933 to 1936 he had worked as deputy to Colonel Wilhelm Wimmer, who oversaw the testing and procurement of the Luftwaffe's first two generations of aircraft. Von Richthofen's brilliance and operational competence was combined with a strong streak of ruthlessness and an intolerance for slowness. Those characteristics would be needed in leading combat operations where rapid decision-making and efficient staff work made the difference between victory and defeat.

From the start the Germans had an effective, if sometimes rocky relationship with General Franco. The Legion Condor commander and chief of staff had immediate and direct access to Franco, and several times they had some strong disputes with Franco, objecting to his slow and methodical approach to fighting the war. But Franco was also a professional soldier and the German and Spanish leaders respected each other on that basis. Franco does not seem to have personally liked the Germans, but he certainly respected their professional competence. And the Germans respected Franco as a talented leader and strategist, even if they did not always agree with him. Essentially, the Germans were there to help Nationalist Spain win the war and Germany's limited interest in Spain reassured Franco. Von Richthofen sized up the situation when he arrived in Spain and recommended that Berlin did not commit too much aid to the Nationalists: 'The Spanish have to win this war for themselves.' Franco mainly agreed.

Franco and the German commanders had an understanding. They could dispute strategic issues with Franco, but once a decision was made then the Legion Condor would loyally work closely with the Spanish to get the job done. The Germans kept Franco informed of everything the Legion Condor was doing and the relationship between the German leaders and Franco was based on trust.

Yet there was certainly some friction between the Legion Condor commanders and some of the Spanish generals. Although most of the professional officers of the Spanish armed forces had gone over to the Nationalists, many in the Spanish officer corps were ageing, tired, lazy and possessed little serious professional knowledge. From the performance on both sides it seems that many of the Spanish officer corps had joined the army to find a sinecure and were not up to the rigorous demands of modern warfare. Only a few officers had Franco's long record of combat leadership. Some generals, such as Mola, had to be given senior positions due to their political following. General Alfredo Kindelan, chief of the Nationalist Air Force, had played a key role in drumming up support for Franco among the officer corps. In von Richthofen's assessment, carefully recorded in his diaries and reports, many of Spain's generals were useless.

One of the primary problems with the Nationalist high command was the low level of military skills and knowledge possessed by so many of its senior military officers. For example, von Richthofen found General Kindelan to be an 'old used-up fellow'. Yet Sperrle

Luftwaffe signallers in Spain laying telephone wire, summer 1936. Spain was a poor country with limited modern communications infrastructure. The first Germans sent to Spain had to set up the basic operational infrastructure at their assigned bases. (Author's collection)

and von Richthofen had an eye for talent and found many of the Spanish commanders and staff officers to be quite capable. The Germans would then work through the competent officers, regardless of their rank. Major Sierra of General Kindelan's staff was regarded as being especially effective and von Richthofen noted, 'I'd work with him anytime' – a comment which would have been about the highest praise von Richthofen would have given a German officer.

The Germans worked in support of General Yagüe's corps on several occasions and found him to be a first-rate commander. The Germans worked well with General Davila, commander of the Army of the North in 1937 and 1938. The Germans' favourite Spanish officer was Colonel (later General) Juan Suero diaz Vigón. Vigón was capable, intelligent and energetic and a first-rate general staff officer. Vigón and the Germans served together for much of the war. Vigón was General Mola's chief of staff for the Northern Campaign of 1937, and from July 1938 onward he served as Franco's chief of staff. Vigón was very friendly with the Germans and developed a close personal relationship with the German senior officers. Vigón had a tough and ruthless streak that the German commanders appreciated. As Mola's chief of staff in the Basque campaign, when brigade commanders did not move quickly enough or lead their troops effectively, they were quickly relieved. Early in the war a lot of incompetent commanders had to be weeded out and Vigón was a man to do it.

Some of the Spanish generals resented the special access to Franco that the Germans had. For his part, General Kindelan would have preferred to fight the war without the Germans telling him how to best run air operations. But Franco found the German advice to be invariably sound and, as long as the Germans did not get involved in internal Spanish politics, their advice was welcome. The German senior officers met with the Nationalist high command and the staff of the field army regularly, and worked with army and corps staffs on a daily basis. The two groups quickly developed a cordial relationship. Von Richthofen had served as Germany's first air attaché to Italy in 1929–32. He spoke Italian fluently and quickly learned Spanish, although at first he had to communicate in a strange kind of Italian/Spanish military vocabulary which the Spanish found amusing – although they understood it and appreciated von Richthofen's efforts.

Early German operations

While Nationalists and Republicans were waging an often-merciless ground war, combat air operations were kept at a small scale for the first four months of the war due to the small size and obsolescence of the two Spanish air forces. When the Nationalist revolt began the Spanish Air Force and Navy had about 300 aircraft of all types (including trainers) on the books, but virtually all were obsolescent and many in poor repair. The Spanish Air Force had possessed a large variety of aircraft in 1936, the most common being the 90 Bréguet 19 two-seaters, capable of short-range reconnaissance or light bombing. The Bréguet 19 had first flown in 1921. The air force had some Nieuport 52 fighters, another 1920s design, and five De Havilland Dragon bombers and some Dornier Wal bombers. The Republic had some lumbering twin-engine French Potez 54 bombers and their best fighters were a few Dewoitine D.372s. By the start of August, the Republicans had about 200 aircraft and the Nationalists about 100. There were about 200 aircraft in the country that belonged to the national airline or to private owners and both sides commandeered civilian aircraft for their air forces. Spain had a small aircraft industry, CASA, that licence-built foreign designs. The largest aircraft factory at Getafe, near Madrid, fell to the Republic and another assembly plant at Cadiz fell to the Nationalists. Unless foreign aid came, the Nationalist and Republican air forces could do little more than fly reconnaissance missions and nuisance raids.

After the attack on the *Jaime I* the Germans readied their small He 51 squadron for combat and moved the unit to Salamanca to support the Nationalist air units. On 23 August the German He 51s escorted the Nationalist Ju 52 bombers on a mission to attack Getafe airfield near Madrid. With Mussolini also committed to helping Franco, some Italian aircraft also arrived for the Nationalists, the most important of which was the Fiat CR.32 biplane fighter, one of the top fighters of the era. As the Nationalist Air Force grew in capability with German and Italian aircraft and training, the Germans continued to provide assistance. German He 51s supported General Yagüe's column in its successful drive on Talavera in September, the main role of the He 51s being bomber escort. By the end of September, the German He 51 squadron had shot down 19 Republican aircraft (seven Bréguets, four Nieuport 52s, seven Potez 54s, and one Vickers Vildebeest). However, the Germans were also finding out that their sleek He 51, which they believed was a fine machine, was not superior to a Hawker Fury or a Dewoitine D.372 fighter. Still, as the Nationalists drove slowly on Madrid more aircraft arrived to reinforce the Nationalist coalition, including He 59Es, He 60s, a single He 50 dive bomber and two Hs 123s, designed as dive bombers. The German fighter squadron was expanded as well.

Legion Condor officially formed

At the end of October, as the Nationalists were approaching the suburbs of Madrid, the announcement of the expanded German commitment to Spain was made. This expanded force in Spain would be called the Legion Condor and, as it was envisioned, it would consist of a staff, a bomber group of three to four squadrons, a fighter group of three to four squadrons, a reconnaissance group of two squadrons, a seaplane squadron, a communications battalion, a logistics supply battalion, a medical detachment, and an extra-large flak battalion that would have eight batteries (five batteries of 88mm guns, two batteries of light 20mm and 37mm anti-aircraft guns, one battery for training Spanish personnel). The Legion Condor would also attach small flights of prototype aircraft for combat testing with the reconnaissance, fighter or bomber groups, including the latest pre-production models of German aircraft. The army would provide a small tank battalion and a small detachment of military advisors to run training schools for the Nationalist officers and army units.

In the meantime, the Soviet Union was also sending military forces and hardware to Spain and, as the Nationalist cause had been saved by the timely German airlift, now the Republic would be saved, at least for a time, by the arrival of Soviet help. In September Joseph Stalin ordered his armed forces to support the Spanish Republic and to send not only equipment, but a corps of Soviet pilots, armour specialists and military advisors. In October aircraft, tanks, artillery and Soviet military personnel arrived in Spain, and air units equipped with some of the most modern aircraft in the world were being assembled.

In October the Nationalists began bombing Madrid in preparation for an advance into the city. On 30 October Getafe airfield was hit hard by a Nationalist air attack and by 6 November the two armies were fighting in the suburbs. On 4 November the Nationalist coalition met its first Soviet fighters in the air, and it was a severe shock. The Soviets had sent a contingent of experienced pilots to Spain and had assembled two squadrons of Polikarpov I-15 fighters. The Germans found the Russian biplane fighter was far faster and better armed than the He 51 and outclassed it in every respect. The only thing that prevented the Nationalist coalition from being driven from the Madrid skies was the Fiat CR.32 fighters that had arrived with the Italian Air Force units, some of which had been given to the Nationalists. The CR.32 was a fast and nimble aircraft and roughly equal to the I-15. However, when the I-16 monoplane fighter was committed to the battle around Madrid in

November, it quickly proved to be the best fighter in Spain. On 29 October, a strong force of Soviet T-26 tanks appeared in Madrid; similarly, this was an armoured force that outclassed anything the Nationalists had on the battlefield. Soviet SB-2 bombers, one of the best light bombers in the world at the time, also appeared over the Madrid front. The SB-2s were far superior to the Germans' improvised Ju 52 bombers. The Soviet-supplied and -piloted (there were at least 300 Russian pilots in Spain by this time) squadrons began a campaign against the Nationalist airfields.

The Soviet fighters drove away daytime bombing raids and shot down several German, Italian and Spanish aircraft. With the arrival of Soviet tanks and artillery, as well as thousands of enthusiastic foreign volunteers (mostly members of the Communist parties of various countries and organized into the International Brigades), the Nationalist advance was stopped cold. The Republic had won air superiority in the Madrid sector. The He 51 had proven so ineffective against the I-15 and I-16 that it was withdrawn from fighter duties and was to serve as a ground attack aircraft instead. Inadvertently, it was a benefit for the Nationalists as the He 51 turned out to be very effective in that role.

Winter would mostly be a time for building up the new Legion Condor and absorbing the new equipment being sent from Germany. The Nationalists would try again in January, February and March to break into Madrid from other directions, each time being stopped by Republican counter-attacks after making minor gains. The Legion Condor played a useful role in supporting the Nationalists on the river Jarama east of Madrid in February, but the advantage in the air still belonged to the Republic.

In an attempt to break the stalemate on the Madrid front, the German, Italian, and Nationalist air units began a bombing campaign against Madrid between 18 and 22 November. This was not the first attempt to bring strategic bombing into the conflict in Spain. In the early months of the war both sides had carried out some relatively minor raids on each other's cities. However, the raids against Madrid in 1936 were the most significant example of strategic bombing in Spain to date. On 30 November the Nationalist bombing of Madrid inflicted a total of 244 civilian dead and 875 wounded. Still, although the bombing raids on Madrid had little effect on the war or on the morale of either side, they gained the attention of the world's press, with dozens of international journalists covering the war from Madrid.

The bombing of Madrid was soon called off, partly because night bombing was inaccurate and day bombing was far too dangerous for the Nationalist bombers in the face of Republican/Soviet air superiority. By December 1936 on the Madrid front, the Nationalists found themselves unable to fly except in large formations and under heavy fighter escort.

The Republican Air Force, now well-equipped with its modern aircraft and Soviet pilots, provided a demonstration of the decisive effect that air power could have on the modern battlefield. In March 1937, the Republicans counter-attacked a motorized corps of Italian troops at Guadalajara north of Madrid. The Italian air units were grounded by weather and the Republican Air Force threw 125 new fighter aircraft, mostly Soviet-piloted, against the rear of the large Italian column strung along the roads. A corps of 50,000 troops was quickly routed – largely by the effects of Republican air power. The Italian Army lost 500 killed, 2,000 wounded and 500 taken prisoner, with an estimated 1,000 vehicles and 25 artillery pieces destroyed, mainly by air attack. The impressive Republican victory at Guadalajara was one of the most dramatic examples of the era of what air power could accomplish on the battlefield. The Italians were, for a time, completely discredited by their poor performance at Guadalajara.

General Sperrle and Franco photographed in early 1937. Sperrle set a precedent providing strategic direction for the Condor Legion and working directly with Franco and his general staff. This allowed his chief of staff von Richthofen to run the operational planning and direction. Sperrle was no diplomat, but he worked well with Franco and the Spanish leaders. (Author's collection)

CHRONOLOGY

1931

Spanish monarchy ends. King Alfonso XIII forced into exile. Republic is proclaimed. A left-wing majority elected to the Cortes. For the next five years Spain will be torn by constant violence between extremes of left and far-right.

1932

A coup by some army generals is suppressed.

1933

Lawyer José Antonio Primo de Rivera establishes a quasi-Fascist, rightist political party, the Falange.

1934

October A rightist coalition wins the election. The government brutally crushes a miners' strike in Asturias using the army. Out of power, the Socialist Party becomes increasingly revolutionary.

1936

January–June General strikes and insurrections spread. A group of army generals under the leadership of General Mola prepare plans to seize power.

February Elections are held. Spain is fairly evenly divided between extremes of right and left, with little in the middle. The Left Coalition won the elections with 4.2 million, to the rightist National Front's 3.8 million, and only 680,000 voters voted for the centre parties.

13 July Republican assault police arrest and murder the leader of the Monarchists in the Cortez. This provides the Spanish Rightists with their justification to start the coup.

17 July A junta of army officers, including Generals José Sanjurjo, Emilio Mola, and Francisco Franco, call for the army to revolt and seize power throughout Spain. General Franco flies to Morocco and takes command of the colony and Spain's Army of Africa in the name of the junta. In Madrid and Barcelona, military garrisons rise against the government but are defeated when the government arms unions and militia forces.

23 July Days into the revolt, Spain is divided into enclaves, with most of central Spain and Catalonia remaining in government hands along with Asturias and the Basque region. In the north, the coup was largely successful, with Galicia, Old Castile, León and Navarre all falling into rebel hands. In southern Spain, there is an enclave around Cadiz and Seville where the Nationalist coup was successful, and in North Africa and Spanish Morocco the Nationalists take control.

25 July General Franco sends two German businessmen, Adolf Langenheim and Johannes Bernhardt, as his personal representatives to ask for aid from Hitler's government. Langenheim and Bernhardt meet with Hitler in the evening of 25/26 July, presenting their request for German support. Hitler orders the Luftwaffe to prepare to support Franco's army.

26 July Luftwaffe Commander-in-Chief Hermann Göring orders General Helmuth Wilberg to organize a staff and begin sending aid to Franco's Nationalists.

27 July Ten Ju 52 transports are flown through Italy to Spanish Morocco to start ferrying Franco's Army of Africa to Seville. The airlift will last until October and is the first major airlift operation in history. From late July through October, more than 1,200 soldiers a week are flown from Morocco to Seville via German transports. German transports also bring equipment and weapons.

Early August The first Army of Africa troops flown to Seville are organized into a column to strike west and north to clear Republican forces away from the Portuguese border, and to unite the Nationalist southern enclave and army with the northern enclave and army.

31 July The freighter *Usaramo*, with ten Ju 52s, six He 51 fighters, and 85 Luftwaffe personnel, mostly officers and technicians, departs for Spain. The *Usaramo* arrives at Cadiz on 8 August.

14 August Spanish North African troops under General Yagüe take Badajoz on the Portuguese border. Now the Nationalist enclaves in northern Spain and in southern Spain are united. With more reinforcements arriving from Africa in late August, the Nationalist forces reorganize and turn east and start advancing towards Toledo and Madrid.

August and September German weapons, supplies, and aircraft as well as a small military staff are dispatched on more than 20 freighters to Spanish Morocco and southern Spain, to bolster the Nationalist cause. By the end of September, the German forces in Spain will number more than 600 troops. Since the beginning of August, the German forces commited to supporting Franco have been under the command of Major Alexander Scheele.

September Joseph Stalin decides to support the Spanish Republic's government and authorizes the immediate dispatch of Soviet aircraft, tanks, war materiel and advisors to the Republic. By late September, the first Soviet advisors have arrived. By October, Soviet aircraft, tanks and artillery have landed in Republican harbours and are rushed to the defence of Madrid.

September–October Thousands of international volunteers, mostly organized by national Communist parties, arrive in Spain and are organized into International Brigades to fight for the Spanish Republic.

1 October The Nationalist junta becomes a Nationalist state, with a government organized and proclaimed in Burgos, with Francisco Franco as Head of State.

October Nationalist forces advancing with German air support take Toledo, and several Nationalist columns begin moving on Madrid from the west. By late October, Nationalist forces have reached the outskirts and the battle for Madrid begins. German and Spanish Nationalist bombers bomb Madrid.

30 October The Legion Condor is officially proclaimed. In October 1936 the German government decides to commit a larger, but still limited German force to Spain. The answer is the Legion Condor, with approximately 100 aircraft and 5,000 personnel to support the Spanish Nationalist cause. *Generalmajor* Hugo Sperrle is named Commander of the Legion Condor. *Oberstleutnant* Wolfram von Richthofen becomes the Legion Condor chief of staff. On 23 November, because of the strong Republican resistance, supported by Soviet tanks and Soviet aircraft as well as international brigades, the Nationalists stop their offensive on Madrid.

6 November Germans encounter Republican aircraft supplied by the Soviet Union and flown by Soviet pilots. These I-15 and I-16 fighters are far superior to the Germans' He 51 fighters, and the Nationalists soon gain air superiority over the battle front around Madrid. The battle of Madrid continues with violent fighting into the suburbs, but the Nationalist advance is halted by the end of November.

December Nationalists conduct offensives northwest of Madrid and in the south to expand their territory. Italian troops land at Cadiz. The Italian government under Mussolini expands its support to the Nationalists.

1937

6–27 January Nationalists conduct an offensive on the Jarama river, southeast of Madrid. After small advances, the Nationalists are stopped.

March The Republicans win a major victory in defeating the Nationalist Italian attack on Guadalajara. The Republican Air Force's Soviet pilots rout the Italian divisions near Guadalajara with massed air attacks, sending them into retreat. It is one of the first examples of the effective use of airpower for battlefield interdiction.

March With stalemate in the Madrid area the Legion Condor, now reinforced with new aircraft, will be committed to an offensive in northern Spain to first destroy the Basque enclave. The Legion Condor will support General Mola's Army of the North and redeploys its headquarters to Vitoria Airfield in northern Spain.

30 March The Nationalist Army of the North begins its advance into the Basque country towards Bilbao.

4 April The Legion Condor demonstrates the extremely effective use of airpower at Ochandiando where German He 51s and bombers prove very effective in breaking Basque defences. In April 1937 the advance continues through the Basque region towards Bilbao.

26 April The Legion Condor bombs the Basque town of Guernica, drops 32 tons of bombs, destroys part of the town but not the Renteria Bridge that was the main target. The Legion Condor considers the attack successful, with the important crossroads of Guernica closed to the retreating Basque forces for 24 hours. However, Mola's Nationalist Army fails to advance quickly enough. Guernica falls only on 30 April.

May The advance continues, now towards the heavily fortified lines around Bilbao.

11 June The Nationalist Army, with the Legion Condor commanding the Nationalist air units, begins its attack to break through the strong fortifications called the 'Iron Belt' around Bilbao. Heavy air attacks precede Nationalist breakthrough forces.

14 June A breach in the Iron Belt is widened, and some Legion Condor squadrons fly up to seven sorties a day as Basque resistance is broken.

19 June Bilbao, one of Spain's most important industrial cities, falls to the Nationalists. The Legion Condor prepares to continue the campaign to the west to eliminate the Republic's enclave at Asturias.

7 July Republicans initiate a massive offensive at Brunete, west of Madrid. After the initial advance is first slowed, and then halted by the Nationalist forces, the Legion Condor reorients and is moved south to the Madrid area, where it takes command of German and Italian air units to fight the Republican offensive at Brunete. The Legion Condor will command over 200 Nationalist aircraft. Initially the Republicans win air superiority, but after a few days the tide turns. Legion Condor flak guns play an important part in stopping Republican tanks. The Nationalists turn to a counter-offensive, and the Legion Condor now wrests air control over the front from the Republican aircraft, partly thanks to the employment of its Bf 109 squadron, which proves superior to the best Republican fighter, the I-16. Legion Condor attacks on Republican logistics and supplies prove especially effective.

24/25 July The Brunete campaign ends with Nationalists having driven back the Republican offensive. The Republicans suffer heavy losses at Brunete.

August The Legion Condor again moves north, with their target now being Santander. In mid-August the offensive against Santander begins and on 26 August, Santander falls.

September–October The Legion Condor works with Nationalist and Italian forces in a successful offence.

21 October The last Republican stronghold in northern Spain at Gijon falls.

Late October The Legion Condor is reoriented to move to the Madrid area. At the end of October, General Sperrle returns to Germany and General Volkmann becomes Legion Condor commander. Von Richthofen stays until early February 1938 to support Volkmann in the transition.

December The Republicans launch a major offensive against the Nationalists at Teruel and Aragon. The Legion Condor supports the Nationalist defence at Teruel, and then the counter-attack. From December until the end of February, the Legion Condor will fly missions in the Teruel campaign. With poor weather, heavy snow, and cold temperatures, the Legion Condor has to cope with very difficult conditions and does so successfully.

1938

22 March From Aragon the Nationalists launch a major offensive east and south with four corps towards the Mediterranean coast, intending to cut off Catalonia from the rest of the Republic. The advance continues rapidly once the Republican lines are broken. The Republicans are exhausted by the Teruel campaign and the Nationalists make major gains. The Nationalists reach the Mediterranean at Vinaroz on 15 April and divide the Spanish Republic.

April Volkmann recommends that Franco drive north and take advantage of the disorganized state of the Republican forces in Catalonia. This good advice is rejected. Franco decides to drive south towards Valencia.

April The Legion Condor is reoriented to strike south towards Valencia, the Republic's capital, which is the new focus of Nationalist efforts.

April–late July The Legion Condor supports the Nationalist Army's drive on Valencia. The Republicans mass their best forces and conduct a highly effective defence. Despite good air support from the Legion Condor, the Nationalists make only moderate advances with heavy casualties. This is one campaign that resulted in failure for the Nationalists and the Legion Condor. At this point, upset with the slow pace of the war and the impending international crises, Volkmann requests that the Legion Condor be withdrawn from Spain.

25 July Having received new aid, aircraft, tanks, and equipment from the Soviet Union, the Republican

Army in Catalonia has reorganized and with 120,000 men, but little air support, launches a major offensive by two army corps across the Ebro river to take Gandesa and then advance to Zaragoza. At the very least, the Republican Army of the North expects to force the end of the Nationalist offensive against Valencia. In the first two days of the offensive, some Republican units advance 25 miles, but by 6 August, the Republicans are forced onto the defensive. The Legion Condor is redeployed to support the Nationalists' campaign in the battle of the Ebro, which becomes one of the decisive battles of the war.

August–16 November The Nationalists will carry out a series of offensives, eventually pushing the Republicans back across the Ebro river. In three-and-a-half months of fighting, the Legion Condor plays a key role in the close air support of Nationalist forces, and also in interdicting Republican communications and transport. Major targets of the Legion Condor are the Republican Army bridges and ferries across the Ebro river. By mid-November both sides have taken heavy losses, about 40,000 men each. However, the Republican Air Force suffers very heavy casualties in the campaign, casualties that cannot be replaced.

1 November General Volkmann returns to Germany and Wolfram von Richthofen, now promoted to major-general, takes command of the Legion Condor. After a period of reorganization and refitting, the Legion Condor is ready to support the last major Nationalist offensive of the war, which begins on 23 December from Aragon, east and north into Catalonia.

1939

January With effective support from the Legion Condor attacking Republican airfields and interdicting Republican movements, the Nationalists capture Tarragona on 7 January and enter Barcelona on the 27th.

February Nationalist forces reach the French frontier on 9 February and Republican Spain is now reduced to the enclave around Valencia and Madrid to the south. The Legion Condor moves south to support a final offensive on Madrid.

March Republican leaders initiate peace negotiations with the Nationalist government. Republican resistance is quickly collapsing.

27 March The Legion Condor conducts its last mission, bombing Republican troops near Madrid.

28 March Nationalist troops enter Madrid.

1 April Nationalist troops enter the Republican capital of Valencia. Franco declares the end of the war.

April–May The Legion Condor is redeployed to Germany. In July 1939 the Legion Condor has a grand parade and review in Berlin, where the Legion Condor veterans march in their Spanish uniforms and are recognized for their achievements by Hitler.

ATTACKERS' CAPABILITIES
The Luftwaffe, Legion Condor and Nationalist Air Forces

The Heinkel He 70 was developed in the early 1930s as a civilian fast-mail and light passenger plane. The Luftwaffe acquired the He 70 and modified it as a light bomber and reconnaissance aircraft. It performed adequately in those roles. (USAF Historical Research Agency)

When the Spanish Civil War began, the Luftwaffe had been in official existence for only 15 months, having been announced to the world as a new arm of the military in May 1935. Germany after World War I had been forbidden to have an air force, as it had been forbidden to have tanks or modern weaponry, and was limited to an army of only 100,000 men and 4,000 officers. However, one of the key lessons of World War I was that a modern air force was necessary to succeed in modern warfare. By 1918, Germany, like all the major powers, had developed a large air force capable of conducting a wide variety of missions including strategic bombing, air superiority, and army support. This experience was not lost as the restrictions of the Versailles Treaty pushed the German Army to create a secret air force staff and training programme so that when the hated Treaty was eventually renounced, and Germany allowed to rearm, it would have a solid foundation ready to build an air force.

From 1920 until Hitler's accession to power in 1933 the German Army General Staff had developed training programmes for German military airmen, which used civilian flight schools and civilian air companies. The German government's Civil Aviation Office was led and manned by former Imperial Air Service officers who worked closely and secretly with the General Staff to develop civil aviation and German air companies – like Lufthansa – as a secret reserve for the German military. Within the General Staff, an Air Section was developed, and a group of highly talented airmen from World War I were retained by the Army and served as a shadow air force. Germany developed secret training programmes in Russia, with full Russian cooperation, and it also had secret programmes to develop prototype fighters and bombers. Thus, when Hitler came to power, the German Army and Navy had several hundred highly trained and experienced airmen ready to supply the initial air staff and a training cadre for an air force. The Army had even created secret fighter and reconnaissance squadrons by 1932. The prototype fighters and bombers were ready to be put into production and these were equal to the aircraft of the other major air forces in terms of performance. When Hitler came to power in January 1933, it was not a matter of creating an air force from scratch. A solid foundation already existed as well as plans for rapid expansion. It was only a matter of providing the orders and the funds to allow rearmament to proceed – which it did, very quickly.

One of Hitler's first acts as chancellor was to create an Air Ministry, which became a de facto air staff. The army commander-in-chief, General Werner von Blomberg, believed that military success required a strong air force as well as an army, so he directed the General Staff to transfer some of its best officers on the Luftwaffe's general staff. One of the officers transferred was Albert Kesselring, who would win fame as a brilliant Luftwaffe commander in World War II. Another was a man considered the likely future chief of staff of the army, General Walter Wever, who would serve as de facto chief of staff of the nascent Luftwaffe from late 1933 to his death in the summer of 1936 in an unfortunate flying accident.

Along with a group of outstanding general staff officers, the army and navy transferred to the Air Ministry a cadre of several hundred aviation officers and technical specialists that had been retained during the inter-war period. The new Air Ministry also acquired many members of civil aviation who had served in the old Imperial Air Service. With sound leadership at the top, the Air Ministry initiated a large-scale rearmament programme to build a Luftwaffe very quickly. In December 1934 German aircraft factories delivered 160 aircraft a month. Within a year the German air industry would average 265 aircraft a month. In 1936 this increased to 426, and in 1937, 467. A first generation of aircraft had been designed and approved by the Army's shadow Luftwaffe staff in the late 1920s and early 1930s. These included the Heinkel He 51, a standard biplane fighter design for the period, which was of metal frame-and-fabric construction and carried two machine guns. The Germans also had the prototype Dornier Do 11 bomber ready for production, an all-metal monoplane with retractable landing gear.

The first generation of German aircraft had average performance for the time. This did not bother the Air Ministry staff, as even obsolescent planes would serve to train the force in fighter and bomber techniques and provide a means of building up the German aircraft industry, which had languished during the Depression. The first large military aircraft contracts also helped German industry to gain experience in mass production of new models. This approach worked well, as the second generation of Luftwaffe aircraft quickly followed the first and were at the cutting edge of technology: at least equal, and often superior, to any aircraft in the world. The second generation of Luftwaffe aircraft was entering production in 1936 and early 1937 – just as the Luftwaffe was going to war.

Walther Wever, Luftwaffe chief of staff 1934–36. Wever's leadership of the Luftwaffe ensured that when the Germans were committed to Spain, they were well-trained and had a sound doctrine for modern war. (USAF Historical Research Agency)

The Luftwaffe's training programme

Before the Spanish Civil War began the Luftwaffe was already in a mode of rapid expansion. It had grown from a force of 18,000 personnel in March 1935 to over 70,000 by the summer of 1936. Rearmament proceeded apace in terms of both receiving aircraft and graduating trained personnel. Thanks to careful planning before Hitler's accession to power, the Luftwaffe was able to quickly expand and still maintain a high quality of personnel. From its start as an independent service, the Luftwaffe had a two-to-three-year officer training programme built on rigorous intellectual and physical standards, and equal to air officer training programmes of the major powers. General Wever, a product of the rigorous army General Staff course, also insisted on creating a full array of higher officer courses for the Luftwaffe. The Luftwaffe

An 88mm flak gun being towed to a forward position by half-track. All units of the Condor Legion were motorized, allowing flak, signals and logistics units to deploy rapidly to different fronts. (Author's collection)

began a three-year General Staff course in 1935 and developed an innovative programme that combined military history and academic study of airpower with the study of aviation engineering and technology. Like the Army General Staff course, the Luftwaffe General Staff programme included extensive operational exercises and wargames.

However, the General Staff course was a programme for a small group of elite officers who would move on to high command. To have an effective air force one needed a course for all mid-ranking officers that ensured that squadron, group and wing commanders and staffs understood and were well-practised in operational doctrine and in planning and executing air missions. In 1935 the Luftwaffe opened the Luftkreisschule (Air District School) in Berlin for mid-ranking officers, mainly captains and majors, who underwent an intensive four-month course that emphasized doctrine and operational command and planning. Officers from the three main branches of the Luftwaffe – Flying officers, Signal officers and Flak officers – trained together and worked as teams in the many exercises and wargames the Luftkreisschule required. With up to three iterations a year, hundreds of officers were run through the school every year. The graduates would then be moved on to command squadrons and groups and serve on operational staffs.

The director of the school was *Generalleutnant* Helmuth Wilberg, a General Staff officer who had commanded large air forces in World War I and in the 1920s had served as the commander of the shadow Luftwaffe on the army staff. Having learned to fly in 1910 and holding Imperial Pilot's Licence number 26, there were few officers in the world with more knowledge of air warfare. Under Wilberg's direction, all the officers of the Luftwaffe received a thorough grounding in doctrine. Wilberg, a consummate staff officer, would play a central role in the success of the Legion Condor.

The rangefinder for the 88mm heavy flak gun. The Luftwaffe sent some of its newest equipment to Spain for testing under field conditions. (Author's collection)

Luftwaffe doctrine for modern operations

The Luftwaffe published a comprehensive doctrine of air warfare in 1935. The doctrine was developed under the direction of General Wever, who wanted the whole Luftwaffe to be imbued with a common concept of aerial warfare. Luftwaffe Regulation 16 *Luftkriegführung* (*Conduct of the Air War*) was the development of German air war thinking since the 1920s. At its core was a doctrine for continental air war where the air force would carry out both independent strategic missions and also conduct joint operations with the army and navy. Strategic bombing was recognized as a core mission, and the doctrine mandated a strong capability to strike vital industrial and military targets deep in the enemy homeland. However, the other core mission of the air force was what the Germans called 'the operational air war', in which the air force would operate alongside the army in the context of a grand operational plan. In war the first job of the air force was to win air superiority by attacking the enemy airfields and driving the enemy fighters out of the sky. Once air superiority was achieved the air force would seek out key operational targets behind the enemy lines, especially logistics and transport systems, in order to cripple the enemy's movement of troops and supplies. Finally, the air force was to operate in close proximity to the front, attacking key military targets. In offensive operations the air force was to be used in mass and at the decisive point that both the army and air force leaders agreed upon. The doctrine mandated close coordination of the air force with the army. The air force was to be commanded and controlled by airmen but would act with the army in the context of achieving joint objectives.

Ensuring effective joint operations was an important theme for General Wever. In 1935 and 1936 he directed the Luftwaffe to carry out extensive manoeuvres with the army employing the concepts of the new doctrine. A top priority set by Wever was air liaison officers who would be detached to army units, usually division and corps headquarters, with the task of maintaining close communication with the operational air headquarters. Air divisions and corps normally set up headquarters alongside the army corps and armies they were supporting. This allowed the commanders and staffs to coordinate operations and planning and to react immediately to any developments at the front. General Wilberg, who during the previous world war had used the armoured German ground attack planes in mass against key objectives with considerable success, insisted that supporting the army was one of the primary missions of an air force. Wever's long service on the army staff gave him an appreciation for joint operations. With its command emphasis on army–air force cooperation, as well as the routine training of Luftwaffe and army units together on manoeuvres, the Luftwaffe's doctrine was far ahead of other air forces in terms of combined-arms thinking. Thanks to a thorough officer training programme, the Luftwaffe's officers had a better understanding of joint operations than any other air force in the world in 1936. This would make a key difference in the Spanish Civil War.

As the Luftwaffe was expanding very rapidly in 1936, providing moderate support to the Spanish Nationalists in the form of an elite air unit with 5,000 personnel and a few hundred aircraft (many considered obsolete and being replaced with more modern models) was not an undue burden. From over 70,000

This Rheinmetall 20mm rapid-fire light flak gun was used by the Condor Legion in the defence of its airfields and also in direct support of ground troops. It was effective in both roles. (Author's collection)

personnel in mid-1936 the Luftwaffe had grown to 178,000 in mid-1937. By August 1939 the Luftwaffe fielded more than 4,000 modern combat aircraft and had more than 400,000 personnel, or 900,000 with reserves on mobilization. Because of General Wever's emphasis on standards and training, Luftwaffe officers and enlisted personnel were as well-trained as airmen of any major power. Indeed, it was the Luftwaffe that was the best trained air force in Spain. The ethic of thorough German training, which was passed onto the Nationalist airmen and soldiers trained by the German military trainers and advisors, gave the Nationalists an important edge over the Republic's forces by the mid-point in the war.

As the Condor Legion grew to full strength in the winter of 1936/37, one of the first duties of the Signal Battalion of the Condor Legion was to set up airfield navigational aids – even at rough forward airfields. (Author's collection)

Legion Condor organization and development

Unwilling to send a significant ground force to Spain, the decision was made to provide German support in the form of an expanded force which was now given the name of Legion Condor. The Legion Condor would have a unique organization, and would consist of approximately 5,000 military personnel. The Legion Condor would have a headquarters and operations staff company, and its operational parts would consist of a reconnaissance group entitled A/88, which would consist of three nine-plane flights, including both short- and long-range reconnaissance aircraft. The bomber force of the Legion Condor, called Kampfgruppe 88 (K/88), would consist of three or four bomber squadrons. The fighter force would be Jagdgruppe 88 (J/88) and consist of three or four squadrons of fighter aircraft, each squadron with nine aircraft. The Legion Condor's flak battalion Flakgruppe 88 (F/88) was the Legion's largest unit, with more than 1,400 men. It was organized into four heavy and two light batteries of flak guns. A naval reconnaissance squadron that would carry out specialized naval reconnaissance and bombing operations was organized as AS/88. The Legion Condor had a considerable number of support units that would include LN/88, which was the Legion Condor's Signal Battalion, which contained a radio company, a telephone company, an aircraft warning company, and an airfield control company. MA/88 was the munitions depot of the Legion Condor and P/88 was the aircraft park and maintenance unit. In addition to all of these units, which would constitute the equivalent of a small air division, there was also a medical battalion as well as a field hospital, plus some special organizations attached, including a special staff for testing new bombers, a special staff for testing new fighters, and a weather station. In addition, there would be a number of personnel specifically assigned as liaison staff to German and Spanish units. The air attaché and his staff would also come under the Legion Condor.

Aircraft of the Legion Condor

In fact, the war in Spain was welcomed by many in the Luftwaffe's leadership as being an opportunity to test doctrine, organization and equipment in battle. By 1936 the first generation of Luftwaffe aircraft was quickly being superseded by the second generation, which had been developed out of the aerial rearmament plan of 1934. Among these aircraft were some of the most successful aircraft of World War II. The Bf 109 fighter had been first flown in 1935, and this aircraft was an exponential leap forward in terms of fighter aircraft technology and capability: an all-metal aircraft with retractable landing gear, it offered strong firepower and a superb weapons platform, highly manoeuvrable and very capable at high altitudes. In less than two years it went from prototype to production, an astoundingly rapid development. Also among the Luftwaffe's second generation of aircraft was the Heinkel He 111 bomber, which could cruise at over 250mph, carry more than 1,500kg of bombs, and operate at high altitudes – an exponential leap forward from the relatively primitive Ju 52 modified transports that equipped most of the Luftwaffe bomber squadrons in its first years. Other aircraft coming on stream included the Ju 87 Stuka dive bomber, which would play an important role in World War II. The Dornier Do 17 could be equipped as a long-range high-altitude aerial reconnaissance aircraft or as a fast light bomber. It served very well in both roles.

The Heinkel He 45 was a late 1920s design that belonged to the first generation of Luftwaffe aircraft. The He 45 was used as a light bomber and short-range reconnaissance aircraft. He 45 production had ended in summer 1936, when the He 46 came into production. Surplus to Luftwaffe needs, the He 45s were sent to the Condor Legion and also equipped Nationalist Air Force squadrons. (USAF Historical Research Agency)

In the early days of the Legion Condor, the primary reconnaissance aircraft was the Heinkel He 45, which was a very conventional, fabric-covered, two-seater biplane that had first been manufactured in 1932. At a relatively low speed of 155mph, it could carry a load of light bombs. One of the more advanced aircraft of the Legion Condor was the Heinkel He 70, an all-metal monoplane that had first flown in 1932. With a top speed of over 200mph, it was faster than the He 51 fighter. The Luftwaffe had ordered a large number of He 70s in 1934. These aircraft were capable of serving as light bombers, carrying 300kg of bombs, but their main role was to serve as high-altitude, long-distance reconnaissance aircraft. Because of its high speed, the He 70 was able to evade enemy fighters. In November 1936, eighteen He 70F-2 aircraft arrived in Spain.

The Heinkel He 45 was an obsolescent aircraft and production had already been closed in the summer of 1936. In Germany, the He 45 was being replaced by the He 46, a high-wing two-seater monoplane that would, in turn, be replaced as the Luftwaffe's short-range

Slightly faster than the He 45 it replaced, the He 46 was used for reconnaissance even though it could also carry 120kg of bombs. Thirty-six He 46s went to Spain and equipped Condor Legion and Nationalist squadrons. (Author's collection)

FRANCE

MEDITERRANEAN SEA

Bay of Biscay

ATLANTIC OCEAN

PORTUGAL

SPAIN

Menorca

Majorca

Son San Juan

Ibiza

100 miles

100km

N

Figueras

Barcelona
Prat del Llobregat

Avispero

Barbastro

Lerida

Tarragona

Reus

Sarinena

Zaragoza

Ebro

Caspe

La Sénia

Calamocha

Villafames
Castellon

Caude

Sarrion
Barracas

Lucena

Valencia
La Senera

Lliria

Rabasa
Alicante

Murcia

San Xavier

Alcantarilla

Los Alcazares
Cartagena

Pamplona

Logrono

Soria

El Burgo de Osma

Barahona

Vitoria

Sondica

Bilbao

Loredo

Villarcayo

Burgos

Carreno
Colunca

Gijon
Siero

Santander

Palencia

Leon

Valladolid

Grajera

Escalona

Segovia

Saachidrian

Avila

Guadalajara

Campo X

Algete
Alcala

Campo Soto
Madrid
Barajos

Cuenca

Campo Robles

San Clemente

Albacete

Toledo

Quintano

Ciudad Real

Valdepenas

Baeza

Jaen

Cordoba

Granada

Taber018

Almeria

Antequera

Malaga

Navalmoral

Arenas S.P.

Talavera

Salamanca

Caceres

Medellin

Merida

Badajoz

Seville

Jerez
Cadiz

Tangier

reconnaissance aircraft by the Henschel Hs 126 in 1938. As the He 45 was going out of service, there were plenty available for the Germans, and some went straight to the Nationalist Air Force, where they served as reconnaissance aircraft and light bombers.

Initially, the mainstay fighter of the Legion Condor was the Heinkel He 51B fighter. This was an early 1930s fighter derived from the Heinkel He 49 of the late 1920s, and it had elegant lines. However, its 550 BMW engine was already obsolescent, and the armament consisted only of two rifle-calibre 7.92mm MG17 machine guns. Although the Germans had a considerable number of He 51s in service, this fighter would soon be replaced by the most important aircraft that the Legion Condor would fly in Spain: the Bf 109 fighter. The Bf 109 was the brainchild of Willy Messerschmitt's small company, the Bayerische Flugzeugwerke, and in 1934, as the first generation of aircraft such as the He 51 and Ju 52 bomber was already filling the units of the new Luftwaffe, Messerschmitt began development of the revolutionary Bf 109. It had its first flight in the summer of 1935, and showed remarkable promise for speed, climb, and manoeuvrability. The first Bf 109 was an all-metal monoplane, powered by a Jumo 210 600hp engine, and equipped with retractable landing gear. In its first trials in 1935, the Bf 109 flew at more than 270mph. Its competitor, the Heinkel He 112, came in at a slightly slower speed. Both the Luftwaffe's second-generation trial aircraft, the Bf 109 and the He 112, were superb fighter aircraft, representing an exponential jump from the fabric-covered biplanes with fixed landing gear common to the air forces of the era. The Bf 109 was not only slightly faster than the He 112; it was also much easier to manufacture. So, it was chosen to be the main fighter of the Luftwaffe, although a number of He 112s were produced for export sales. The first production models of the Bf 109 were completed in December 1936. These were equipped with two 7.92mm machine guns and one variation included a 20mm cannon.

Several of the very first production models of the Bf 109, the B-1, were sent by ship to be assembled in Spain. Although apparently they had arrived by the end of 1936, it took time to assemble the 12 aircraft that had been sent out, and time was also required for several of the top pilots of the Legion Condor to become familiar with flying the aircraft. There were considerable problems in getting the Bf 109s assembled and tested. One aircraft was lost during its trial period and crashed on a ferry flight in February. Still, by the end of February 1937, one flight of Bf 109s was ready for combat and these went to equip the unit's second squadron, 2.J/88. Being a brand-new aircraft, the Bf 109 had a considerable number of engine problems that had to be worked out, but it was clear that the Bf 109 had the potential to change the air war in Spain in the Nationalists' favour.

The Ju 52 bomber, which also served as a transport aircraft, was one of the most distinctive aircraft in the history of the Legion Condor. The Ju 52 had first flown in 1931, and the first models of this rugged, all-metal, trimotor transport with three 660hp BMW 132 engines were sold to Bolivia in 1932, where they gave superb service during the Chaco War as transports capable of operating from small, rugged airfields. It had a crew of three and normally carried 17 passengers. It was a relatively slow aircraft, with a maximum speed of 180mph, and a cruising speed of 155mph. However, because this was already in production when Germany organized its Air Ministry in 1933, it was decided to take the Ju 52 as an improvised, interim bomber, essentially to use it as a means of building and training the Luftwaffe's bomber force until the second generation became available. The Ju 52, as a bomber, carried two machine guns for defence and had a maximum bombload of 1,500kg (with a conversion kit that gave the aircraft three bomb magazines). The bomber wing of the Legion Condor in autumn 1936 consisted of these Ju 52 modified transport bombers.

Another aircraft arriving to equip the Legion Condor was the Heinkel He 111B, which entered production in early 1936. Thirty of the first examples of the He 111 reached Spain in early 1937. The He 111B could fly at 224mph, as fast as most fighters of the era. It was a twin-engine, all-metal bomber powered by DB 600 12-cylinder engines, and the B-variant could carry 1,500kg of bombs. By autumn 1937 K/88 would have two squadrons equipped with Heinkel He 111s. The Ju 52 bombers were transferred to the Spanish Nationalists as the Legion squadrons received new equipment.

Another important aircraft to serve with the Legion Condor was the Dornier Do 17 bomber. The Do 17 first flew in 1934 and was a very fast aircraft for the time. This all-metal monoplane bomber with smooth lines could carry 1,000kg of bombs. In the spring of 1937, one squadron from Germany was deployed to join the Legion Condor in Spain, equipped with 15 Do 17s, which would become the first squadron of the Legion Condor's reconnaissance group. As the Do 17s arrived, the He 70s of the reconnaissance group were transferred to the Spanish. Eventually, both air forces flew the Do 17E model, which carried a slightly heavier bomb load and flew at a top speed of 222mph. The E-model served as bombers and the F-model for long-range reconnaissance.

Naval Air Squadron operations

When the Germans committed to the Spanish Civil War in autumn 1936, the Luftwaffe deployed a small reconnaissance flight of He 59 and He 60 seaplanes. The Legion Condor numbered the squadron AS/88 (Aufklärungsstaffel 88, or Sea Reconnaissance Squadron 88). The Luftwaffe seaplane units were tasked with cooperating with the Nationalist and Italian naval air units, which played an important role in the mission of attacking Republican shipping and harbours. By July 1937, nine He 59 and eight He 60 seaplanes had arrived to give the Germans a full squadron-sized force. The Heinkel He 59 was a large, four-seat, twin-engine biplane seaplane. Although it was a slow aircraft, it had considerable range and could carry 1,000kg of bombs or torpedoes. For defensive purposes it was well armed with two machine guns and a 20mm Rheinmetall aircraft cannon. The smaller Heinkel He 60 was

The gunner in the forward position of an He 59 bomber. (Author's collection)

An He 59 at the seaplane base in Majorca. The base served Nationalist and Italian naval air units. (Author's collection)

a two-seat, single-engine biplane seaplane that served primarily as a reconnaissance aircraft and carried no more than 120kg of bombs. The Legion Condor would employ approximately 15 He 59s and eight He 60 aircraft between 1936 and 1939.

The German seaplane unit normally operated out of Mallorca in coordination with the Spanish and Italian naval air units, but also operated from bases on the Mediterranean coast. In July 1937 a combined German–Italian–Nationalist air staff was established in order to better coordinate the campaign against Republican shipping and ports. In contrast with the friction the Legion Condor experienced when working with the Italians to support the land campaign, the relationship of the coalition naval air units was quite harmonious. The Nationalist coalition seaplane force, although composed of obsolete aircraft, proved to be remarkably successful at anti-shipping and interdiction missions during the war. During the conflict, the Republicans lost 554 ships, mostly to naval action, but 144 to German and Italian naval air units. A further 106 foreign ships that were carrying supplies to the Republic were also sunk by naval aircraft.

As the war progressed, the Legion Condor's naval air squadron advanced from a reconnaissance mission to a specialized mission of attacking shipping inside Republican ports. Attacks at sea, away from the ports, were normally carried out by day. But attacks on the well-defended Republican ports were invariably carried out at night. When attacking ports, the pilots of the He 59s developed a special tactic of cutting their engines and gliding in for the last few miles in silence. Once the bombs had been released, the pilot would restart, give the aircraft full throttle and rush back out to sea. The normal anti-shipping weapon was a 250kg bomb delivered at low altitude, which proved to be very effective. The He 59s became so proficient at night bombing that during the campaign in Aragon and along the Ebro in 1938, the He 59s routinely flew long-range night-bomber missions to attack key Republican railyards and rail junctions supporting the Republican Army. Given its small size and obsolete equipment, the naval air arm had a disproportionately large impact on the war. Nationalist officers who visited Barcelona harbour after the city fell to the Nationalists in 1939 described the great devastation, with 30 ships sunk by air attack in their berths, and many other ships damaged.

The Heinkel He 59. Though slow and obsolescent, this large twin-engine biplane was a very capable aircraft with considerable range. It carried a four-man crew plus three machine guns and one 20mm cannon. The He 59 could carry a variety of bombloads including a 1,000kg torpedo or 1,000kg of conventional bombs. (Author's collection)

Flak battalion

With more than 1,400 men this was the largest single unit of the Legion Condor. Unlike in other armed forces, in Germany the anti-aircraft force was a part of the air force, not the army. Germany had been producing the 88mm heavy flak gun since 1932 and would equip four batteries with this excellent gun. The 88mm flak gun had a vertical range of almost 11,000m, which meant that virtually all the aircraft flying in the 1930s were within easy range of the gun in the anti-aircraft mode. But the 88mm was a versatile design and could also be used in a conventional artillery role. With a range of 14,800m when engaging ground targets, the 88mm gun had a longer range than most army fieldpieces of the era. The F/88 Flak battalion was also equipped with two large batteries of 20mm and 37mm rapid-fire anti-aircraft guns. Like the heavy 88s, the light flak could also be used against ground targets. F/88 had two missions in the war – to protect the Legion Condor's airfields, which it did quite competently, and to support the Nationalist ground troops using their guns in the direct and indirect fire modes. Because the Nationalists lacked artillery, especially early in the war, and the 88mm and light flak guns proved so effective in the ground support role, F/88 saw constant combat in the front lines.

General Kindelan was head of the Spanish Nationalist Air Force, and resented the German commanders' influence over Franco. The Germans, for their part, had little respect for Kindelan. (Sr Vicente Blas)

88mm flak gun set up for airfield defence. The 88mm gun could be set up from its mobile carriage and readied to fire in under four minutes. It was an exceptionally effective heavy anti-aircraft gun and could also be used to engage ground targets. (Author's collection)

A major advantage of the 88mm gun was its mobility. The 88mm gun was mounted on a mobile carriage that could be set up and be ready to fire in under four minutes. The 88s in Spain were hauled by halftracks, which made it possible to tow the gun into rough terrain.

Legion Condor signals battalion

Another large battalion of the Legion Condor was N/88, the signals battalion. The Luftwaffe knew that a modern air force was only effective if it had modern communications, and it tested various radios and vehicles in Spain to ensure that the Luftwaffe had highly mobile communications. Because of the efficiency of the signals battalion, the Legion Condor and Nationalist staffs could set up command posts on the front lines and be fully connected to all the army and air units in the region. The signals battalion was also a fighting unit that saw considerable front-line service. Laying telephone wire and setting up radio stations at forward command posts was dangerous work and the Legion's signallers lost casualties to Republican artillery and small-arms fire.

Legion Condor support units

One of the advantages of the Legion Condor was a highly efficient logistics system. The Legion Condor set up major depots and was able to efficiently assemble, repair and overhaul aircraft. This ensured that even in times of intensive operations, the operational rate of the Legion – which never had more than 120 aircraft – remained high. The aircraft armourers and munitions and fuel support personnel could turn aircraft around quickly. At times of intense combat, such as in the Basque country in 1937 or over the Ebro in 1938, the support troops of the Legion enabled the aircraft to fly four or more sorties per day.

Airmen from the Condor Legion's munitions company handling a 250kg bomb. The 250kg bomb was the standard heavy bomb of the Condor Legion. The efficient support troops of the Legion enabled the bomber and fighter units to fly as many as four sorties per day during intense combat. (Author's collection)

The Germans deployed a small tank battalion with two companies of Panzer I tanks to Spain. (Author's collection)

Legion Condor Order of Battle (per summer 1937)

COMMAND AND STAFF (S/88)
SPECIAL UNITS AND STAFF SECTIONS:
Liaison Staff for German and Spanish units (VS)
Air Attaché
Weather Station
Medical Battalion
Field Hospital (Laz 88)
Air Operations Company (B/88)
Park and Aircraft Group (P/88)
Munitions Depot (MA/88)
Bomber Test Staff (VB)
Fighter Test Staff (VJ)
FLYING UNITS:
Reconnaissance Group (A/88)
3x squadrons: 1x with Do 17s (also used as bomber); others flew He 70s and He 46s
Maritime Squadron (AS)
9x He 59 Seaplanes, 8x He 60 seaplanes
Fighter Group (J/88)
3x squadrons (each with 9x aircraft): 2x with He 51 (used for ground attack)
1x Bf 109 squadron
Bomber Group (K/88)
3x squadrons (with 9x planes each): 2x with Ju 52s, 1x He 111

OTHER BATTALIONS:
Flak Battalion (F/88):
4x heavy flak batteries (88mm flak guns), 2x light flak batteries (mix of 20 and 37mm rapid-fire flak guns, 1x battery for training Spanish units)
Signal Battalion (N/88):
1x aircraft warning company, 1x airfield control company, 1x radio company, 1x telephone company
Army Units in Spain:
Under Spanish military command but received logistics and administrative support from the Legion Condor
1x Panzer Battalion (about 200 men):
2x companies of Pz I tanks, 1x support company
Small army training teams with Nationalist Army

The Luftwaffe sent 15 He 59s to Spain. The He 59 was also very useful in the night bombing role. (Author's collection)

While the Nationalist coalition looked like it vastly outnumbered the Republicans in the air, for most of the war that was not the case. What the Legion Condor and Nationalist logistics could do was to make much better use of the few aircraft they had.

The Nationalist Air Force

Like the air force of the Republic, the Nationalists improvised a small air arm in the first weeks of the civil war. General Alfredo Kindelan had been one of the army's first aviators, but he had not been involved in aviation since his resignation from the military in 1931. In some ways Kindelan was a competent leader. He oversaw the creation of an air force school system. While most of the aircraft remained in the Republic's hands in July 1936, the Nationalists did have control of the major air depots at León and Seville. Kindelan was able to effectively use the aircraft industry in Nationalist territory to repair and refurbish aircraft and he set up contracts to licence-build German trainers at Cadiz.

The Nationalists were dependent upon obtaining German and Italian aircraft in the same way the Republic depended upon the Soviet Union. From the start of the war the Germans and Italians provided training teams to the Nationalists. By May 1937 the Nationalist Air Force had one fighter group equipped with He 51s and one of Fiat CR.32s. By that date the Nationalists also had five reconnaissance/light bomber squadrons, some equipped with the venerable Bréguet 19, but being re-equipped with the He 45 and He 46. The Nationalists also had two groups of Ju 52 bombers with a third bomber group in the process of receiving the Italian SM.79.

While the Nationalists could not truly compete with the Republic's air force in mid-1937, a year later the Nationalists had a powerful and mature force. In the summer of 1938, the Nationalist bomber units were receiving He 111s and Do 17s from the Germans and

The Hs 123 was tested in Spain early in the conflict. The Luftwaffe supplied enough for the Nationalists to create a squadron. This rugged biplane would go on to serve as a close-support aircraft throughout World War II. (USAF Historical Research Agency)

In late 1938 the Germans supplied the Nationalists with 17 He 112s, enough to equip a fighter squadron. The He 112 was close in performance to the Bf 109. (Author's collection)

SM.79s from the Italians – all first-rate aircraft. While the mainstay of the Nationalist Air Force was the CR.32, with the He 51s relegated to close support duties, by the end of 1938 the Nationalists were ready to field squadrons equipped with the He 112 and the Bf 109. In mid-1938 the Nationalists reorganized their air force into four air divisions, with a total of 450 combat aircraft.

Working with the Germans

For much of the war the Nationalist squadrons operated under German operational command, a situation certainly resented by General Kindelan, but which the Spanish airmen appreciated. The officers and men assigned to the Legion Condor seemed to have worked hard to demonstrate sensitivity, understanding and goodwill towards the Nationalist soldiers and airmen. The Legion Condor commanders set a Luftwaffe tradition by regularly visiting the Spanish units at the front to observe close air support operations. Junior officers of the Legion Condor attempted to learn Spanish and also visited the Spanish units at the front. The Germans developed a special affinity for several of the units of the Nationalist army, in particular the Navarrese and Moroccan divisions that they regularly flew support for. Luftwaffe personnel also developed a close working relationship with the Nationalist Air Force and combined missions were common events. Captain José Larios, Duke of Lerma and Nationalist fighter ace, regularly flew missions with the Legion Condor. Luftwaffe reports often praised the combat performance of the Nationalist Air Force units. In 1938, when the Legion Condor had a shortage of pilots due to the European war crises, General Volkmann filled out the German bomber crews with Spanish aviators – which not only kept the German units up to strength, but also gave the Spanish experience in operating the He 111. Gone were the complaints of August 1936 that the Spanish pilots could not effectively fly German aircraft. The Legion Condor reported that the Spanish learned to fly the He 111 very quickly – a tribute both to the Spanish training system and Legion Condor tutelage.

The Italian Air Force

Due to the nature of Italy's strategy and the ambitions of its dictator, Benito Mussolini, the Spanish–Italian relationship was not as smooth as with the Germans. Italy had an agenda to become the lead Mediterranean power and demanded that Franco give Italy bases in return for Italian help. The Mussolini government pushed Italy's pretensions to be a major military power and sent 70,000 troops and more than 5,000 airmen to Spain. While the Nationalists appreciated the Italian aid and support in the desperate first months of the war, the Nationalist attitude changed when Italian ground troops arrived in Spain. First of all, Franco had never asked for ground troops. When the Italians arrived General Roatta, commander of the Italian Volunteer Corps, failed to brief Franco on Italian military operations or intentions. For the whole of the war the relationship with the Italians was very rocky.

Still, the Italians sent a large air corps to Spain, more than 200 aircraft, and this made a big difference at key points in the war. In late 1936 and early 1937 the Nationalists would have been driven completely from the skies over central Spain if not for the Italian fighter units armed with CR.32s. In some campaigns the Italians cooperated very well and played a major role, notably in the campaign that overran Aragon in the spring of 1938. During the course of the war the Italians supplied more than 700 aircraft to the Nationalists, compared with the German contribution of 650 aircraft. As with the Germans, some of the Italian aircraft given to the Nationalists were older models, but some of the aircraft supplied were the newest models of the Italian Air Force, including the SM.79 bomber.

The 37mm flak gun, along with the 20mm flak gun, equipped the light flak batteries of the Condor Legion. (Author's collection)

DEFENDERS' CAPABILITIES

The Republican Air Force

The Soviet-made I-15 first flew in 1933 and entered production in 1934. It was a gull-winged biplane armed with four rifle-calibre machine guns and fully equal to the other biplane fighters of the early 1930s that were the mainstay of all the major air forces. It was equal to the Nationalist Fiat CR.32 fighters and superior in performance to the German He 51s. The first I-15s arrived in Republican Spain in October 1936 with Soviet pilots. By January 1937 the Republican Air Force fielded four full-strength squadrons of I-15s. (Sr Blas Vicente)

At the beginning of the war about 150 Spanish Air Force pilots sided with the Republic. By August 1936 the Republic's air force had about 200 aircraft on the books, the most common type being the very obsolete Bréguet 19 two-seater. The rest of the inventory contained a bewildering variety of aircraft including some Potez bombers and license-built Nieuport 52 fighters, both slow and ungainly craft. The Republic had a handful of reasonably effective fighters in the form of a few Hawker Furies and some Dewoitine D.372s, both fabric-covered fighters dating from the early 1930s.

The commander of the Republican Air Force, General Hidalgo de Cisneros, was a nobleman who had joined the Communist Party. As a Communist he was eager that the Republic win the support of the Soviet Union. In terms of leading the Republican Air Force, he performed well in putting together a good training programme. However, the Republican Air Force lacked a coherent doctrine for fighting. In some set-piece battles it performed well, but the Republic mostly flew in defensive operations and left the initiative, and resulting control of the air, to the Nationalists.

Of the Soviet military personnel who served in Spain, the largest number belonged to the Soviet Air Force. The Soviet Union sent some of their most experienced officers to serve as senior advisors to the Republican forces. The head of the Soviet airmen in Spain was Colonel Jacob Smushkevich, codenamed 'General Douglas'. He got along well with Cisneros, a fellow Communist, but had a reputation of being disdainful of non-Communists. General Goriev became the primary Soviet advisor in Madrid and General Kulik was assigned as the Republican Central Front advisor. Like the Germans, some of the notable World War II Soviet aces and ground force commanders gained their first war experience in Spain. Future Soviet marshals Malinovsky, Rokossovsky and Konev all fought for the Republic, and the largest single contingent of Soviets in the war was the 772 airmen. Only a few thousand Soviets in total served in Spain, but they were able to man whole air groups and tank units. Soviet advisors also set up military schools for the Republic's forces. Hundreds

of Republican pilots were sent to Russia for training and special schools were set up in Republican Spain as well.

As most of the Spanish aviation infrastructure had remained in Republican territory, the Republican Air Force was able to arrange for Soviet aircraft to be built under licence in Spanish factories. The Republic also had an infrastructure of workshops and depots.

By the end of November 1936 there were 300 Soviet pilots in Madrid. Most of the large Spanish gold reserve of $500 million had been transferred to the USSR in October 1936 and it purchased a considerable amount of the latest military hardware. The first aircraft to arrive were the SB-2 fast bombers, a twin-engine all-metal monoplane with a three-man crew. The SB-2 was armed with three machine guns, could carry 550kg of bombs, and had a 900-mile range. Flying at 250mph it was faster than almost all the fighters of the day and it was fast enough not to need an escort. Also arriving in October were the Soviet Air Force's two main fighter aircraft, the Polikarpov I-15 and the Polikarpov I-16.

The I-15 was 60mph slower than the I-16, but with four machine guns and high manoeuvrability it was a formidable fighter plane. (Sr Blas Vicente)

The I-15 was the main fighter of the Republican Air Force. More than 250 were imported from the Soviet Union and a further 287 built under licence in Spain. (Sr Blas Vicente)

The Polikarpov I-16 represented a huge advance in fighter design. The Soviet Union sent 276 of these fighters to the Republican Air Force between 1936 and 1938. This monoplane had retractable landing gear and later models reached a top speed of 326mph. When the I-16 first appeared over the front it far outclassed all the best German and Italian fighters and, with the I-15s, won air superiority for the Republicans from autumn 1936 until the spring of 1937. (Sr Blas Vicente)

The first I-16s suffered from a light armament with only two machine guns. The modified I-16s that flew for the Republican Air Force in 1938 had four machine guns. The fighter could carry up to 500kg of bombs. While fast and highly manoeuvrable and with a good climb rate, its design made it highly unstable and a difficult aircraft to fly. Many were lost to operational accidents when flown by inexperienced pilots. (Sr Blas Vicente)

The I-16 was one of the most advanced fighter aircraft in service in the mid-1930s. A monoplane of mixed metal-and-wood construction with retractable landing gear, the light and stubby-looking fighter was manoeuvrable and very fast for the time with a top speed of 282mph. The only drawback was its light armament of just two machine guns. However, when it arrived in Spain it was easily the best fighter in the country and was the main reason for the Republic gaining air superiority in November 1936 and holding it through early 1937.

The older I-15, known as the *Chato*, was a biplane single-seat fighter with a gull-wing design and a top speed of 220mph. The I-15 handled nicely and carried four machine guns. It was one of the top biplane fighters of the day and was far superior to the He 51. Until the Bf 109 arrived the only Nationalist aircraft that could match the I-15 was the Italian Fiat CR.32.

The Republican Air Force relied primarily upon the Soviets for aircraft and Soviet supplies ensured the Republicans had a fairly balanced force. One of the first aircraft to be supplied

to the Republic was a shipment of 31 Polikarpov R-5 reconnaissance/light bombers. The R-5, a metal-framed fabric-covered biplane known as the *Rasante*, fulfilled the role of a short-range reconnaissance craft. As a late 1920s design it was already obsolete and was being replaced by the Polikarpov R-Z. The newer Polikarpov design was also a biplane but with a sliding canopy for the pilot and an 820hp engine. Capable of 196mph and armed with three machine guns and able to carry 400kg of bombs, the R-Z (or *Natascha*) was used extensively in the ground-attack role as the slower and older R-5 was relegated to the night bombing role.

The Tupolev SB-2 light bomber first flew in 1934 and had just entered serial production in 1936 when the Soviet Union sent 36 to the Republic in October 1936. This three-seat, all-metal aircraft was one of the most advanced bombers of its day. It carried a light bomb load, only 600kg of bombs, but with a top speed of 263mph it was faster than the German He 51 or Italian CR.32 fighters, and thus very hard to shoot down. (Sr Blas Vicente)

Foreign volunteers for the Republic

The most notable foreign volunteers for the Spanish Republic were the International Brigades, which consisted mostly of Communist Party members from all over Europe (France, Germany, Poland, the UK, and Italy) with a contingent of Americans and Canadians as well. The foreign volunteers began arriving in September 1936 and, after brief training, were committed as national units and brigades to the battle around Madrid from November 1936 to March 1937. Approximately 30,000 volunteers served in the International Brigades, which became elite units of the Republican Army and played a major role in the war.

But the International Brigades were not the only foreign volunteers in Spain. In the summer of 1936 French writer and political activist Andre Malraux mobilized a group of anti-Fascist volunteers to form an air group to go to fight in Spain. Malraux's effort won a lot of positive publicity for the Spanish Republic. Malraux, who was not a pilot, was given the rank of lieutenant colonel and allowed a free hand to create his air unit, answerable only to General Cisneros. Equipped with 70 obsolescent aircraft that France agreed to sell to Spain (including some ancient Bréguet 19s), the grandly named *Escuadrilla España* contributed

The R-5 was the main reconnaissance aircraft/ light bomber of the Soviet Air Force in the early 1930s. Thirty-one were sold to Spain and arrived in October 1936. The late 1920s design was obsolete by the Spanish Civil War so the Republican Air Force relegated this plane to night-bombing missions. (Sr Blas Vicente)

The Soviet Air Force put the R-Z into production as a replacement for the R-5. It was faster and carried an armament of three machine guns and could carry 400kg of bombs. The 90 R-Zs of the Republican Air Force were mainly used in the groundattack role. (Sr Blas Vicente)

little to the Republic's defence. Some of the aircraft obtained for the Spanish were so old and in such poor repair they were considered death traps by the pilots who would fly them. The *Escuadrilla España* flew a few missions, and never made much of a military impact. The unit was disbanded in February 1937 and the remaining aircraft were taken into other squadrons.

Other enthusiasts came to fight for the Republic motivated by other reasons. In December 1936 six American pilots with previous military flight training arrived in Spain. They had been promised large sums to fly and a bonus in gold for each aircraft shot down. The American volunteers were first issued some old aircraft that, like Malraux's pilots, they recognized as death traps and refused to fly. Within weeks most of the Americans returned to the United States. However, a few non-Soviet foreigners won fame flying for the Republic as mercenaries. Frank Tinker, an ex-US Navy pilot, negotiated a huge salary of $1,500 a month and a $1,000 bonus for each aircraft shot down. Tinker was credited with eight kills during the war and survived the conflict. The foreign pilots flying for the Republic added a sense of romance to the conflict, but aside from the occasional skilled pilot like Tinker, accomplished little.

During the war the Russians supplied 657 aircraft to the Spanish Republic, mostly very modern designs. The numbers break down as: 92x SB-2 bombers; 161x I-15 fighters; 276x I-16 fighters; 31x R-5 reconnaissance bombers; 93x R-Z reconnaissance bombers; 4x UT 1 trainers. In addition, the Republic licence-built 230 I-15s and about 100 I-16s. The Republic was able to import about 150 foreign aircraft during the war. Given the Russian support with equipment and training for the Republican Air Force, it cannot be said that the Republic lacked the means to fight a modern war. However, with a few exceptions, the Republic mostly fought defensively for most of the war, where the Nationalists and their coalition allies used their aircraft far more aggressively.

The SB-2 bomber was the mainstay of the Republican bomber force. Enough had arrived in autumn 1936 to allow the Republican Air Force to form Bomber Grupo 12 (initially with Soviet pilots and aircrew). Camouflage was important as airfields were primary targets for both the Nationalist and Republican air forces. The first SB-2 mission in Spain was the bombing of the Nationalist airfield at Seville on 28 October 1938. (Sr Blas Vicente)

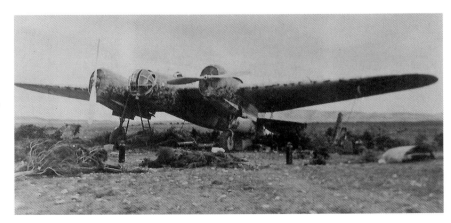

THE CAMPAIGN
The Luftwaffe's expeditionary war

The Basque country, spring 1937

When the Nationalist offensives against Madrid failed in early 1937, Franco looked for a vulnerable point in the Republic's defences. The Republican Army, bolstered by the International Brigades and Soviet aircraft and equipment, held the advantage on the Central Front. However, the Republican enclave in the north – the Basque provinces and Asturias – were largely cut off from supplies and reinforcements from the rest of the Republic and were a highly vulnerable target. With the Legion Condor commanders fully agreeing with the new strategy, Franco transferred some of his best divisions and much of the Nationalist Air Force to the Northern Army under General Mola.

The offensive was slated to begin at the end of March, with the Basque country and its capital of Bilbao being the main objective. The Legion Condor would command the Nationalist air units on the front and the Italians would participate as well. Mola had over 100,000 well-armed Nationalist troops who faced Basque forces approximately 45,000-strong and another 60,000 Republican troops in Asturias. However, the Basques and Asturians did not cooperate well and the Nationalist coalition would have an advantage in artillery, supplies, and especially airpower.

In March 1937 the entire Legion Condor deployed to northern Spain – to the airfields in the Vitoria area – and General Franco gave the Legion Condor responsibility for all air operations in the theatre, which meant that Spanish Nationalist squadrons came under German control. When the Legion Condor deployed to the north it had approximately 100 operational aircraft, supported by two to three Nationalist air squadrons. This gave the Nationalist coalition forces over 150 aircraft in the northern sector. To oppose the Nationalist Air Force and the Legion Condor, the Basques had a mere handful of aircraft. During the spring campaign the Republican government sent a force of ten fighters to reinforce the Basques, which required them to fly across Nationalist Spain. Only seven of them arrived and the Republic gave up further attempts to reinforce the Basques by air. The Republic had a few dozen aircraft in Asturias, but nowhere in the north could the Republic put up a real showing in the air.

The He 111 first flew in 1935 and production began in late 1936. The first He 111s were sent to re-equip the Condor Legion bomber units. With a bombload of 2,000kg and a top speed of 242mph as well as modern features such as a variable pitch propeller, the He 111 was the best medium bomber in the world at that time. The excellent performance of the He 111 enabled it to effectively strike strategic targets (ports, railyards, factories) deep in Republican Spain. (Author's collection)

The Ju 52 was the Condor Legion's main bomber from summer 1936 to autumn 1937. During 1937 the Ju 52s were replaced by He 111s. The Ju 52s were turned over to the Nationalists, although the Condor Legion staff retained some as transport planes. (Author's collection)

The Legion Condor had spent the winter of 1936/37 expanding from a few hundred personnel to a force of more than 5,000. While organizing the full force and developing sound logistics, aircraft maintenance and support systems, the Legion Condor received some of Germany's newest military aircraft to put into combat. The Legion Condor received the first production models of the Bf 109 fighter and the He 111 bomber. The Bf 109s had arrived at the end of 1936, but not only had they taken considerable time to assemble, they then had to be tested and pilots trained on the Bf 109, which was a very different type of aircraft to the He 51. The He 111 also had teething problems. However, by the onset of the Basque region offensive 2.J/88 was being equipped with Bf 109s. While the Ju 52 remained the main bomber of the Legion Condor, the He 111s would equip the squadrons as they became available. Some of the first models of the Do 17 also arrived, which were initially used as a light bomber (it had roughly the same capabilities as the Republican SB-2), but as more He 111s became available the Do 17s would be tasked as long-range reconnaissance aircraft, a role they were especially suited for. The main base of the Legion Condor would be Vitoria, close to the Basque region, but some of the bombers would be based in Avila.

While Sperrle and von Richthofen were preparing for the offensive they were also having to contend with some considerable friction with the Nationalist northern commander, General Mola. After Franco, Mola was the most important Nationalist commander because he commanded a large following among parts of the Nationalist political coalition. However, he was a problematic leader. Whatever Mola's political talents, he was no match for Franco as a strategist or military commander. Mola had commanded the offensive on Madrid in October and November 1936 and had failed to take the city. In October he bragged on a radio broadcast that the four army columns advancing on Madrid from the west and south would not take the city – it would be the fifth column of Nationalist supporters inside Madrid that would do so. This led the Republican government to begin mass house-to-house searches and initiate a witch-hunt for likely Nationalist supporters. More than 2,000 suspected Nationalists were rounded up and summarily executed. Although there were indeed many people in Madrid hoping for a Nationalist victory there was no organization that would lead them to rise up against the government. Mola's radio boast led the Republic to slaughter many innocents.

The Basques were good at building fortifications – which is why the Condor Legion bombers and flak guns were needed to blast open a way for Nationalist soldiers. (Author's collection)

When Mola took command in the north he surprised and shocked Sperrle and von Richthofen by insisting that the Legion Condor employ its bombers attacking the factories of Bilbao. The German commanders thought such a policy was frankly lunatic and told Mola so. Sperrle and von Richthofen argued that it was nonsense to bomb valuable industries that they hoped to occupy very soon. But Mola insisted that the Legion target Bilbao factories because Spain had too much industry and he believed a postwar Spain ought not to be dominated by the industries of Barcelona and Bilbao. Sperrle went to Franco to establish a policy that no factory would be bombed by the Legion Condor unless Franco granted his express approval. After some debate one of Mola's targets was eventually approved – a munitions factory – but the German commanders placed the approved target at the bottom of their list of priorities and promised Mola to carry out the bombing as soon as bombers could be freed up from the constant missions against the Basque front lines.

Despite being outnumbered and outgunned by the Nationalists, the Basque Army had the advantage of enthusiastic troops who held mountainous terrain and strong defensive lines

A close strike by a heavy bomb has shattered the concrete of this emplacement so that only the reinforcing bars (a.k.a. 'rebars') remain. Throughout the war the Condor Legion carried out careful studies of the effects of German bombs and munitions on a variety of targets. (Author's collection)

Avila

EVENTS

Republican offensive, 7–11 July

The Republican V Corps with five divisions carried out the main effort on the Republican left flank, attacking south to the crossroads town of Brunete. The V Corps' left flank was covered by the XVIII Corps with four divisions. Once Brunete fell, the Republican advance would head east to link up with the Republican II Corps (two divisions) advancing west from the southern suburbs of Madrid.

If successful, the two pincers of the Republican offensive would encircle six Nationalist divisions in a shallow salient west of Madrid. The loss of 60,000-plus troops and their equipment would be a major blow to the Nationalist cause.

With artillery and air superiority, and strong superiority in ground troops, the Republicans made some initial rapid advances but became bogged down by islands of Nationalist resistance such as Villanueva de la Canada. The Republican attack from the Madrid suburbs got nowhere. Reacting quickly, the Nationalist government halted its offensive in the north and shifted divisions to reinforce the threatened sector. A day into the offensive, the Condor Legion was redeploying squadrons towards Madrid to deal with the emergency. Condor Legion light flak batteries made it to the most threatened sectors of the Nationalist lines and stiffened their resistance.

By 11 July the Republican units of General Miaja had advanced several kilometres east of Brunete, but the Nationalist reinforcements and the Condor Legion's redeployment to the central front stabilized the situation and the Republicans could go no further.

Condor Legion interdiction attacks

From the start of the campaign the Condor Legion employed its bombers to strike Republican supply depots behind the lines. Republican depots at El Escorial, Collado Villalba, Manzanares el Real, Colmenar Viejo, Matallana, and San Agustin de Guidalix were repeatedly bombed and road traffic strafed by the He 51 fighters. Supply problems caused by the interdiction strikes slowed down the Republican momentum.

First Nationalist counter-offensive, 18–22 July

The reinforced Nationalists carried out attacks on the flanks of the salient the Republicans had created, in the hope of cutting off their forward divisions. In a series of bloody battles, the Nationalists managed to make some gains on their right flank, but attacks on the left flank made no progress.

By the end of the first week the Nationalists, with the Condor Legion in the lead, had managed to win air superiority over the battlefront — largely due to the appearance of the Bf 109, which was clearly superior to the Republic's I-16 fighter. The Condor Legion was over the front daily, searching for targets on the front lines.

Second Nationalist counter-offensive, 23–26 July

The main objective of the second Nationalist counteroffensive was to break through the centre of the Republican salient at Brunete and drive towards Villanueva de la Canada. Nationalist forces were redeployed with the 13th Division making the main effort towards Brunete and the 34th Division supporting its right flank. The town of Brunete fell on 24 July, and the Republicans fell back to a low hill with a cemetery, 1km north of Brunete. The high ground dominated the terrain north of Brunete and the elite Republican 11th Division had prepared a formidable defence with deep trench lines; they were supported by two artillery pieces and T-26 tanks.

At 1400hrs on 25 July, the 13th Division attacked the cemetery position with two regiments. The Condor Legion used all available bombers and fighters in a maximum effort to provide air support for the attack. As the attack began, the Republican defences at the cemetery were pounded by heavy bombs. As the Nationalists advanced across the open ground, flights of He 51s flying in relays made low-level bombing and strafing attacks to target any heavy weapons and to keep the Republican infantry deep in their trenches and dugouts. Thanks to the Condor Legion's relentless and accurate attacks, the Nationalist regiments were able to advance without undue casualties and overrun the Republican defences. The Nationalists continued the advance for another 4km and by the day's end had taken Hill 662. This battle and the advance of the Nationalist 34th Division effectively ended the Brunete campaign. This final Nationalist effort left the Republicans with only a small piece of territory gained since the initial advance of 7 July.

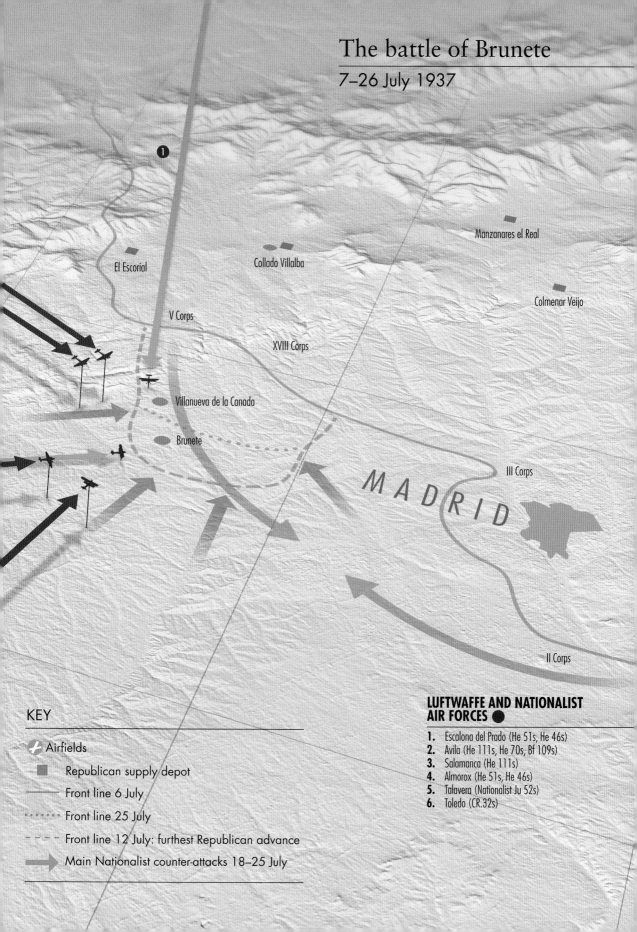

The battle of Brunete
7–26 July 1937

Manzanares el Real

Collado Villalba

El Escorial

Colmenar Veijo

V Corps

XVIII Corps

Villanueva de la Canada

Brunete

III Corps

M A D R I D

II Corps

KEY

✈ Airfields

◼ Republican supply depot

— Front line 6 July

······· Front line 25 July

- - - Front line 12 July: furthest Republican advance

➡ Main Nationalist counter-attacks 18–25 July

LUFTWAFFE AND NATIONALIST AIR FORCES ●

1. Escalona del Prado (He 51s, He 46s)
2. Avila (He 111s, He 70s, Bf 109s)
3. Salamanca (He 111s)
4. Almorox (He 51s, He 46s)
5. Talavera (Nationalist Ju 52s)
6. Toledo (CR.32s)

around Bilbao. The Basques had also shown some talent in building fortifications. There could be no rapid Blitzkrieg through the Basque country. The Nationalists would have to pry the Basques out of their successive defensive lines in a series of set-piece attacks. Sperrle and von Richthofen saw their mission as supporting the Nationalist Army on the offensive and using all their capabilities to break the Basque defences without incurring excessive casualties for the Nationalists. While army cooperation was always an important mission for the Luftwaffe, the Legion Condor would have to develop tactics that suited the situation. The Legion Condor had already flown army support missions, but on a fairly small scale. Now they would have to plan for much larger scale air/ground operations. The Nationalist Army was not trained to work in close cooperation with the air force, so in the Basque country the Nationalist commanders and troops would have to learn quickly. Dealing with an army inexperienced in modern combined-arms warfare, the Legion Condor would have to teach the Nationalist army and air force how to fight a modern campaign.

The key problem to be overcome in the campaign in Vizcaya Province (the Basque region) was how to effectively coordinate the army and air forces to break through the Basque defences. The Legion Condor staff and the staff of the Nationalist Northern Army would carefully plan each step in the campaign. Aerial reconnaissance would pick the best location for the attack. Army units would be brought close to the jump-off point and their positions clearly marked by panels on the ground. Artillery, including the Legion Condor's light and heavy flak guns, would be emplaced and used as part of a coordinated fires plan. Just before the ground attack began the heavy bombers would carpet-bomb the enemy positions. Fighter squadrons would roam the area immediately behind the enemy front, especially targeting artillery positions, road movement, and the small towns that would hold enemy supplies and reserves. Any enemy retreat was relentlessly attacked.

One of the key innovations in the campaign was to set up an observation post for the army and air commanders and their staffs on a hilltop overlooking the point of attack. The hilltop would be connected by phone and radio to ground units and to the main airfields in the rear. There was no means in 1937 for forward ground units to talk directly with the aircraft overhead, but the ground observers were connected to the airfield in the rear by telephone and the rear airfields could communicate with the bombers and relay messages. It was an

Two companies of Panzer I light tanks hardly constituted a *Blitzkrieg* force. But the German tank battalion in Spain was mainly used in the traditional role of supporting the infantry. (Author's collection)

awkward system but it worked. Only in 1941 would ground controllers on the front lines be able to talk directly to aircraft overhead. The coordination of the air and ground forces improved markedly as the campaign progressed. However, despite improved communications and better signals to prevent friendly fire, there were still several instances of German and Italian aircraft dropping bombs on Nationalist infantry in April 1937.

The Germans soon found that a concentrated bombing effort of towns on the front line was a very effective means of supporting the ground troops. On 4 April heavy air attack preceded the Nationalists' ground attack against Basque positions at Ochandiano. Employing all of the bombers of the Legion Condor in mass, the Germans rained 60 tons of bombs down upon the town. After the bombardment the Nationalist ground forces were able to overrun Basque positions with little resistance – finding over 200 Basque soldiers killed by air attack and taking 400 prisoners too dazed to retreat. As Richthofen put it, 'there were many dead and the target was clearly destroyed.' In April, the Nationalists heavily bombed the town of Durango, which was close to the front lines and contained Basque Army reserves and supply points. Again, the bombing had the desired effect of disrupting the Republican defence.

Although Luftwaffe doctrine emphasized the use of air power in mass, one tactic employed regularly by the Luftwaffe in Spain and found to be very successful was the shuttle attack – sending one flight at a time down to drop bombs on enemy positions and then returning to base to rearm and refuel, while the next flight in the squadron took over the attack. Because the Legion Condor bases were close to the Basque front lines, it was possible for the Legion Condor to fly three or more sorties per day on the same objective by May. The tactic of shuttle attacks meant that the enemy could be kept under pressure for hours at a time, which increased the stress and psychological pressure upon an enemy defender. Air power was soon to show some impressive results.

The bombing of Guernica, April 1937

The Legion Condor played the lead role in the single most famous incident of the Spanish Civil War – the air attack on Guernica, a small Basque town located close behind the Republican Army lines. On 26 April 1937 it became the most-written-about single action of the Spanish Civil War.

Guernica was a small industrial town of 7,000 people that had a key bridge and road junction crossing the Mundaca river. It was the only river crossing for 20 miles and a large portion of the Basque Army, 23 battalions, was in retreat to positions behind the river. If the bridge could be cut and the town closed to traffic the main escape route of the Basque Army could be cut. Guernica offered a chance for operational-level interdiction.

At 4.30pm on 26 April, the Legion Condor attacked Guernica. Three modern He 111 medium bombers and one Dornier Do 17 light bomber flew in the lead as pathfinders. They were followed up by 18 Ju 52 bombers and supported by Bf 109 and He 51 fighter planes. The attack was also joined by some Nationalist Air Force Ju 52s. Attacking in waves of three to four aircraft, the Legion Condor's aircraft pounded the town for an hour. The Germans dropped about 32 tons of high-explosive and incendiary bombs on the town, with the Renteria Bridge as the aim point. The initial bombing pass dropped their bombs just short of the bridge. With the target covered in smoke the successive waves of bombers dropped their bombs into the area of the town centre. The bombing raid failed to destroy the bridge, but one end of the town was thoroughly wrecked, and this met the tactical objective of shutting the road to traffic for 24 hours. However, the Nationalist Army, just a few miles from Guernica, failed to move up quickly and trap the Basque Army. During the next three days the Basque Army cleared the road through Guernica and evacuated its forces over the Renteria bridge. Von Richthofen commented that while the raid on Guernica was a 'technical

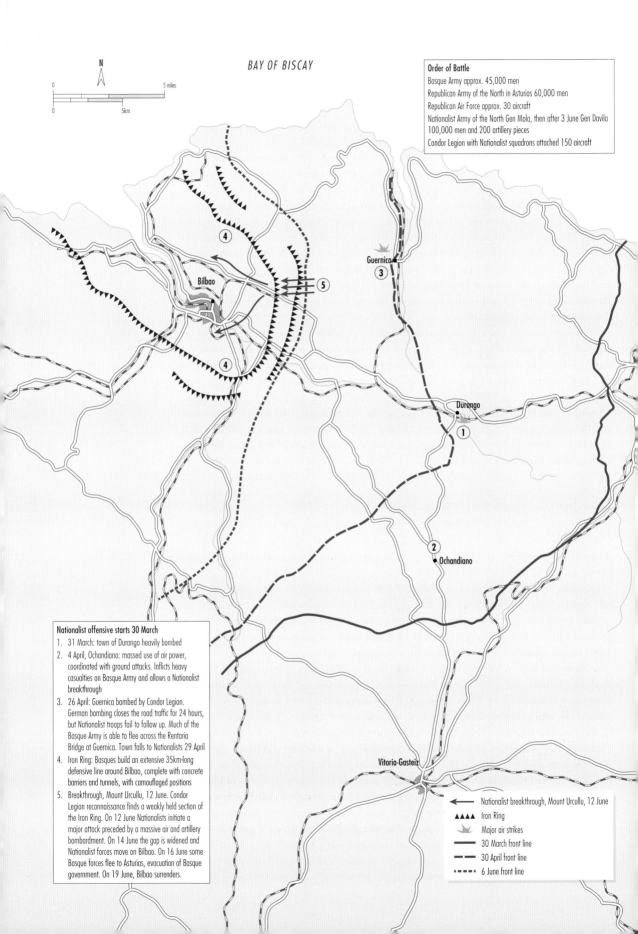

N

BAY OF BISCAY

0   5 miles

0   5km

Order of Battle
Basque Army approx. 45,000 men
Republican Army of the North in Asturias 60,000 men
Republican Air Force approx. 30 aircraft
Nationalist Army of the North Gen Mola, then after 3 June Gen Davila
100,000 men and 200 artillery pieces
Condor Legion with Nationalist squadrons attached 150 aircraft

4

Guernica
3

5

Bilbao

4

Durango
1

2
Ochandiano

Nationalist offensive starts 30 March

1. 31 March: town of Durango heavily bombed
2. 4 April, Ochandiano: massed use of air power,
   coordinated with ground attacks. Inflicts heavy
   casualties on Basque Army and allows a Nationalist
   breakthrough
3. 26 April: Guernica bombed by Condor Legion.
   German bombing closes the road traffic for 24 hours,
   but Nationalist troops fail to follow up. Much of the
   Basque Army is able to flee across the Rentaria
   Bridge at Guernica. Town falls to Nationalists 29 April
4. Iron Ring: Basques build an extensive 35km-long
   defensive line around Bilbao, complete with concrete
   barriers and tunnels, with camouflaged positions
5. Breakthrough, Mount Urcullu, 12 June. Condor
   Legion reconnaissance finds a weakly held section of
   the Iron Ring. On 12 June Nationalists initiate a
   major attack preceded by a massive air and artillery
   bombardment. On 14 June the gap is widened and
   Nationalist forces move on Bilbao. On 16 June some
   Basque forces flee to Asturias, evacuation of Basque
   government. On 19 June, Bilbao surrenders.

Vitoria-Gasteiz

     Nationalist breakthrough, Mount Urcullu, 12 June
▲▲▲▲ Iron Ring
     Major air strikes
——— 30 March front line
– – – 30 April front line
· · · · 6 June front line

success' he was disappointed that the Nationalist Army had not followed up the raid quickly enough and seized the town, and by doing so, cut off the retreat of much of the Basque Army.

The raid on Guernica was similar to many other raids targeting small towns in Spain during the war. The German operational rationale in bombing towns like Guernica was explained in a Legion Condor report to Berlin made on 11 February 1938: 'We have notable results in hitting targets near the front, especially in bombing villages which hold enemy reserves and headquarters. We have had great success because these targets are easy to find and can be thoroughly destroyed by carpet bombing.' In the report, it was noted that attacks on point targets, such as bridges, roads and rail lines, were more difficult, and generally less successful simply because the bombers were not effective in hitting precise targets. The era of precision bombing had not yet arrived.

However, the era of mass media *had* arrived. The Basque government trumpeted the attack on Guernica as a 'terror attack' against a defenceless 'open city' (it was not, there were two Basque Army battalions in the town) with the intention of using massive air strikes to break the will of the Basque population. The government released an official figure of 1,687 dead and more than 800 wounded – almost half the population of the town as casualties. British reporters visited Guernica just after the attack and described scenes of horrific devastation. Lurid descriptions of the bombing were spread on headlines of the major newspapers throughout Europe and America. Pablo Picasso was inspired to paint his great work 'Guernica' which was exhibited at the world exposition in Paris just a few weeks later.

Ironically, a news event written to alert the world to German brutality and gain international sympathy for the Spanish Republic ended up as Hitler's greatest victory in the Spanish Civil War. The wildly exaggerated reports of the bombing (the actual count for civilians killed at Guernica was 300, not 1,687) gave the world the impression that the Luftwaffe could easily raze entire cities to the ground – something certainly not within the capabilities of the Luftwaffe in 1937 or 1938, or even in 1940. The popular story of Guernica was very much in the minds of the British and French governments when British Prime Minister Neville Chamberlain and French Premier Edouard Daladier met with Hitler at Munich in September 1938 and bargained away the freedom of Czechoslovakia, primarily because they and their populations feared the total destruction of their cities by the Luftwaffe.

Final advance and the fall of Bilbao, April–June 1937

The Nationalists advanced slowly through April and May. The terrain was one series of steep hills after another. The weather in May did not cooperate, with heavy rains impeding movement and air operations. The daily planning of air and ground operations was the work of Legion Condor chief of staff von Richthofen and the chief of staff of the Nationalist Northern Army, Colonel Juan Vigón. The two of them and their staffs worked well together as the campaign progressed. Nationalist Army commander General Mola seemed too sympathetic to Nationalist unit commanders who failed to act aggressively and quickly follow the Legion Condor's air strikes with a ground advance. It was up to chief of staff Vigón to relieve commanders who did not perform, a policy that improved the Nationalist leadership and had the full approval of the Germans.

During April and May 1937 the Nationalist Army, with effective air support from the Legion Condor, relentlessly pushed the Basques out of one position after another as the Basque Army retreated towards Bilbao. The campaign in the north for the Legion Condor remained essentially a tactical air campaign, although some missions were flown against

The Condor Legion was at first surprised at just how effective the 88mm gun was in destroying fortifications. (Author's collection)

transportation targets near Bilbao. Although the Basque air defences were weak the Legion Condor found it necessary to escort the Legion bombers with its new Bf 109s, which quickly proved to be the best fighters in Spain – more than a match for any that the Republican forces could send against them. The first Bf 109 victory in combat came in early April when the Legion's Bf 109s on patrol encountered four Republican I-15s and shot one down.

An important part of Luftwaffe doctrine was to use fighters and light bombers to attack road and rail traffic close to the front. (Author's collection)

During the spring of 1937 the Basque Army built an impressive line of fortifications around the major Basque city of Bilbao. The fortifications, called the 'Iron Belt', was actually two lines of fortifications built by engineers and architects, each of which consisted of bunkers and well-made strongpoints, some made of reinforced concrete, and connected by trench lines with machine gun nests sited every 500m. The line was 35km long and extended from northwest of Bilbao completely around the city to the east. Held by a large Basque force, it was in every way as strong a defensive line as had been seen during much of World War

I. By early June the Basque Army had retreated behind the Iron Belt. Since its flanks rested on the sea it could only be neutralized by frontal assault. Because the Nationalist army was deficient in artillery and possessed no significant numerical advantage over the Basque Army on the ground, the Legion Condor was put to work planning an air campaign that could breach the Iron Belt and open the way for the Nationalists to seize Bilbao. Once Bilbao was taken, the Basque resistance would collapse due to loss of supplies and armaments production. The Legion Condor thus put all its resources towards the saturation bombing of vital sectors of the Iron Belt with its heaviest bombs. By this time, coordination of the ground and air forces had improved to the point where air attacks were quickly followed up by ground attacks and the air forces could react to any ground forces' requirements for additional support.

In the middle of the campaign General Mola was killed when his transport plane crashed. Mola was quickly replaced by General Fidel Davila, an older general (he had fought the Americans in Cuba in 1898) but highly respected and trusted by Franco. Davila would be appointed War Minister in February 1938 and would command the field army in key sectors for the rest of the war. Davila would command in northern Spain in 1937, in Aragon in 1937–38 and at the Ebro in 1938.

As the Army of the North approached the Iron Belt fortification line, the Legion Condor's reconnaissance squadron A/88 played its key role in the campaign by carefully photographing the entire Basque defence system. As well as pinpointing the major fortifications and enemy artillery emplacements, they also discovered some weakly fortified sectors in the Iron Belt that could be broken and exploited. The final offensive featured attacks in waves on this key gap in the defences east of Bilbao. The arrival of the F-model Do 17, which was now the main long-range reconnaissance aircraft of the Legion Condor, represented a major improvement in the Nationalist capabilities. The short-range reconnaissance units of the Legion Condor, which were transitioning from the He 45 to the He 46 (with the He 45s being turned over to the Nationalist Air Force as light bombers), also performed well in monitoring the entire Basque line for any movement. The final offensive was based on good intelligence and included not only massive air strikes on the Basque front, but artillery support and the use of the German tank battalion and Nationalist tanks to support the infantry and to pursue the enemy once the line was broken.

Heavy bombing proved devastatingly effective against the Iron Belt and between 12 and 14 June the Legion Condor and the Nationalist Army broke through the Basque defences at Mount Uralla, near the town of Fica. The Legion Condor and the Nationalist Air Force were effective not only in shattering the Basque fortifications but also in preventing the

Condor Legion officers developed a high opinion of the Nationalist infantry soldier, especially the troops of the Moroccan and Navarrese units, who were regarded as exceptional fighters. (Author's collection)

Basques from bringing reserves up to the threatened parts of the line. The Legion Condor bombers and fighters and the Nationalist squadrons assisted the Nationalist divisions in conducting a pursuit campaign against the Basque Army once the breach in the lines was effected. It took three days of heavy fighting to break the 'Iron Belt'.

Five days later, on 19 June 1937, Bilbao surrendered. Thousands of Basques had been evacuated by sea to France, but much of the Basque Army was forced to surrender. Most of Asturias remained in Republican hands, but almost half of the Republic's troops in the north, as well as artillery and considerable materiel, had been lost with Bilbao's surrender. With the fall of Bilbao, the Republic lost one of its major industrial centres and the Nationalists proved that they could inflict decisive military defeats upon the Republican government. It was also a major blow to the morale of the Republic.

The Asturias region was the next objective to be mopped up by Nationalist forces during the summer, but the fall of Bilbao required an operational pause for the victorious Nationalists and the Legion Condor to rest, regroup and replenish supplies. Moving to Asturias would require the Legion Condor to relocate its airfields and logistics to the west.

In the campaign in Vizcaya the Legion Condor had proved that it could adapt to the circumstances of the Spanish Civil War and could effectively coordinate an air-ground campaign and overcome powerful defensive positions. It is no exaggeration to say that the Legion Condor made the Nationalist victory in the north possible. Not only did the Legion Condor and Nationalist aircraft inflict heavy casualties on the Basques and managed to blast defending troops out of carefully-prepared positions, but air power in the interdiction role made it extremely difficult for the defenders to reinforce threatened points and react quickly and in strength to Nationalist ground movements. In short, air power in northern Spain in 1937 not only proved that it had great shock and destructive effects, but also proved that the side possessing air superiority would hold the initiative on the battlefield.

Probably a Navarrese unit. Condor Legion officers routinely visited the Nationalist units they were supporting. (Author's collection)

The battle of Brunete, July 1937

As the Legion Condor was preparing to complete the campaign in the north and advance on Santander and Asturias at the beginning of July, the Republican Army was preparing a major offensive that could potentially change the course of the war in favour of the Republic. In the region just west of Madrid, in a quiet area of the front line, the Republican forces under General Miaja were preparing what was to be the largest and potentially the most important Republican offensive of the entire civil war. Although the Republic was taking a beating in the north, on the central front around Madrid the Republic's forces had been successful in repulsing all Nationalist offensives since October 1936. The army of assorted party and union militias and International Brigades were taking on the appearance of a real army. Training and weapons had improved. Most importantly, the trainers and advisors from the Soviet Union along with the Red Army soldiers who manned most of the tanks and the Soviet Air Force pilots who flew most of the Republican aircraft were solid professionals who were helping to mould the Republican Army. The divisions manned by the Communists were known for their discipline and Communist officers such as General Lister had proven to be capable combat leaders. Yet, while training, organization and equipment for the Republican Army had greatly improved, the Republicans still suffered from leadership problems. As most of the experienced professional officers of the Spanish Army had gone over to the Nationalists, it was hard to build staffs to manage the planning, logistics and support required for large-scale army operations. The strengths and weaknesses of the Spanish Republican Army would become evident in the July 1937 offensive.

The Do 17 was just coming into Luftwaffe service in 1936. It served effectively as a bomber and long-range reconnaissance aircraft. After enough He 111s arrived, the Do 17s were used for reconnaissance. (Author's collection)

With the Legion Condor and some of the best Nationalist units diverted to the campaign in the north, the Republic saw a prime opportunity for a major offensive operation that could inflict heavy casualties on the Nationalists. An offensive west of Madrid offered the Republic the best chance to win a victory that would change the whole military and political situation in Spain. A major Nationalist defeat would demoralize the Nationalist coalition, would encourage the Western nations to more openly support the Spanish Republic, and might force the Germans and Italians to reconsider their support for the Nationalists as a lost cause. The site chosen for the offensive was a large Nationalist salient to the west and north of Madrid. This sector on the Madrid front had not seen any action for months and the front was lightly held by Nationalist troops. The Republicans planned to encircle the salient and surround 55,000 Nationalist troops with an attack with two pincers: one pincer starting just south of Madrid and driving west, and another pincer west of Madrid driving southeast. There were no major river

General Sperrle (centre) with Spanish and German staff officers at a forward command post in the Basque Country, spring 1937. The Germans placed a strong emphasis on command and control and Condor Legion commanders routinely set up forward command posts so that they could observe major air and ground attacks. The Legion's signal battalion set up telephone and radio communications so that the command post could communicate with the army unit headquarters and with the main Condor Legion airbase in the rear. In 1937 it was not possible for the smaller ground radios to communicate directly with the aircraft, so messages were relayed to the Condor Legion's base which did have radio contact with the bombers. (Author's collection)

or mountain obstacles on this sector of the front and, once the front was broken, the terrain favoured rapid movement. The area was well served with roads and rail connections and there were good airfields in the vicinity.

With new shipments of tanks and aircraft arriving from the USSR, and with newly trained pilots and tank crews as well as Soviet advisors flying the aircraft and driving the tanks, the Republican forces put together an attack based upon two corps: the Republican V Corps, consisting of five of the best Republican divisions, and including five International Brigades and supported by more than 130 guns, would carry out the main attack, driving towards Madrid from the western flank. After taking the Brunete crossroads part of the corps would advance south and the main force would swing due west towards Madrid. At the same time the Republican XVIII Corps, with four divisions, and also heavily supported by tanks and artillery and armoured cars, would support the attack on the V Corps left flank. The Vallecas Corps, with two divisions, would advance due west from the southern Madrid suburbs to link forces with the V Corps. If it succeeded the offensive could destroy six Nationalist divisions and two brigades deployed in the shallow salient on the front west of Madrid. Potentially, destroying more than 60,000 Nationalist troops could be a decisive blow to the Nationalist cause.

At the beginning of July, a Republican force with a total of 90,000 troops, more than 160 tanks, and more than 200 guns was deployed to the Madrid area. In the attack sector this Republican Army had decisive superiority in manpower, firepower, and tanks. Moreover, at this point the Republican Air Force could count approximately 400 combat aircraft. A large air force was also assembled in the Madrid sector. When the battle of Brunete began on 6 July General Miaja would have approximately 200 fighters, which were supported by

two groups of Polikarpov R-5 *Natasha* biplanes, as well as two bomber groups of the fast SB-2 bombers – about 300 aircraft in all. There were hundreds of Soviet pilots flying for the Republic at this point. At the opening of the offensive the Republic could count on an overwhelming air superiority.

The initial attack on 6 July took the Nationalist forces by surprise. At the main breakthrough point of the Republican V Corps, the Nationalist forces had only 2,700 defenders, including two battalions of Moroccans who had recently reinforced that sector. Still, despite the overwhelming superiority of the Republican forces, the Republican advance began to bog down very quickly. On the flank south of Madrid, the Republic's Vallecas Corps made its initial attack and was immediately slowed, and then halted by Nationalist resistance and withdrew on the first day back to their starting point. On the other hand, the right sector of the Republican attack, which had massive superiority along the front, broke through the Nationalist front and rapidly advanced. On the first day of the advance the western pincer advanced 16km and on the first evening had encircled the crossroads village of Brunete. General Yagüe, who was commanding this sector of the front, saw the danger immediately and contacted the commander of the Central Army Group and requested that the reserve Nationalist 13th Division be immediately committed to the front. All the available forces that he could find in the Madrid area were thrown in, and Yagüe ordered that the small village of Villanueva de la Cañada, at the axis of the Republican drive, be defended to the utmost. The Nationalists, although greatly outnumbered, were equipped with some very well-manned anti-tank guns that helped hold off the advance of General Lister's division for a full day. The Republic, with a striking advantage in both quality and quantity of tanks, failed to use their armour to drive forward and around the Nationalist islands of resistance.

Yet the collapse of a sector of the Nationalist front caused considerable disorder for the victors. Republican units became intermixed and the attack slowed down as General Miaja and his staff failed to sort out the confusion. Resistance at other points could have been easily bypassed, and in fact as soon as Villanueva de la Cañada fell, the front was generally open to a rapid advance. The whole attack was predicated on using the immediate Republican superiority to cut off the entire salient before Franco could react and reinforce the front.

The poor coordination of the Republican Army gave the Nationalists an opportunity to reinforce the threatened sectors and to pull reinforcements in from the Northern Army. At this point, the weakness of Republican coordination and planning became evident. Despite their superiority, the division and corps commanders of the Republican forces behaved cautiously. Rather than bypass islands of Nationalist

Colonel Juan Vigón of the Nationalist Army. Vigón was an exceptionally talented staff officer and served as chief of staff of the Nationalist Northern Army in the Basque campaign. Vigón worked very well with the German commanders who respected his ability and his grasp of strategy, operational planning and doctrine. In 1938 Franco made Vigón (promoted to general) his personal chief of staff. After the war Vigón served as Spain's air minister. (Author's collection)

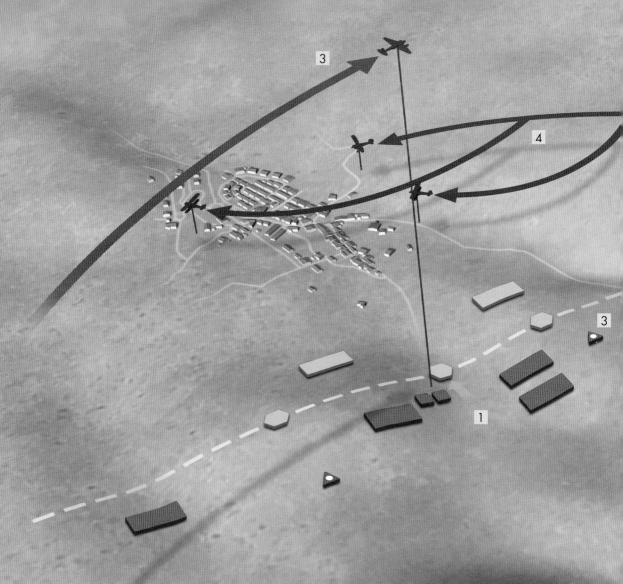

KEY

➡️ Main point of attack

🔺 Condor Legion flak: light and heavy

🔺 Spanish Nationalist artillery: light guns and howitzers

● Condor Legion hilltop command post

▬ Nationalist infantry

⬡ Republican strongpoints

- - - Defended Republican front

▬ Republican infantry

The Condor Legion's method of tactical air support

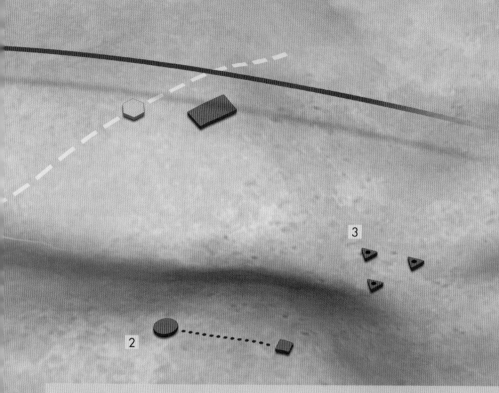

EVENTS

Through 1937 and 1938 the Condor Legion developed a standard method for providing air support to ground offensives. The operation is preceded by intensive aerial reconnaissance by long- and short-range aircraft to identify the enemy unit locations, fortifications, headquarters, supply points, and artillery positions.

1. Armed with this information, the Nationalist commanders and the Condor Legion commander and staff select the best spot for an attack. Condor Legion light and heavy flak batteries are brought forward to support the attack. The light flak will be close to the jump-off point and concentrate fire on the sector to be attacked. The heavy flak will be located further to the rear, along with the Nationalist artillery, and during the attack will concentrate fire on the major enemy strongpoints.

2. A command post is set up for Condor Legion and Nationalist senior commanders and staff officers on high ground overlooking the site selected for attack. The Condor Legion signals battalion ensures there is telephone contact with ground units and also back to the main Condor Legion air base in the rear. While the ground commanders cannot talk directly to the bombers overhead, they can relay messages to the Legion air base, which does have radio contact with the bombers.

3. As the attack begins with German and Nationalist artillery preparation to suppress enemy fire, the site selected for the breakthrough will be blasted by waves of the Legion's heavy bombers to stun the defenders just before the Nationalist infantry, supported by tanks and armoured cars, hits the attack sector.

4. To the immediate rear of the attack sector the Condor Legion's He 51 fighters, as well as He 45s and He 46s (used as light bombers as well as reconnaissance aircraft), and Nationalist fighters and light bombers make low-level bombing and strafing sweeps to attack headquarters, supply depots, artillery and any reinforcements moving forward. When the enemy retreats the supporting fighters will relentlessly attack and harass the forces.

This system, first used in the campaign against the Basques, proved highly successful. Effective air support enabled the Nationalists to break well-fortified Republican positions without undue casualties. This model evolved into the tactical air support methods of the German Army and Luftwaffe that proved equally effective in the 1939 and 1940 campaigns.

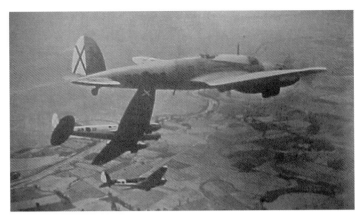

The Condor Legion bomber group was re-equipped with He 111s through 1937, with the Ju 52 bombers given to the Nationalist Air Force or relegated to transport duty. The He 111 first played a major role in the battle of Brunete, where the new German bombers carried out highly effective interdiction attacks against the Republican Army. (Author's collection)

resistance and sweep forward to outflank the Nationalist Army at every point of resistance, the Republicans slowed and even stopped. In the decisive first days of the offensive, with overwhelming Nationalist superiority in the air, on the ground, and in tanks and guns, the opportunity was wasted. In the meantime, General Franco contacted General Sperrle in northern Spain, requesting help from the Legion Condor, which was immediately deployed.

At first thinking that this was a limited attack, the Legion Condor deployed only some of its available forces: the Dornier Do 17 bomber squadron was sent as well as a Bf 109 squadron and as early as 7 July, on the second day of the offensive, the Legion Condor went into action. On 7 July, General Franco, realizing that this was a major offensive and that it posed a great danger to the Nationalist forces, asked for the full support of the German and Italian forces as well as reinforcements from the Nationalist Army fighting in the north. The offensive against Asturias was immediately stopped and the Legion Condor and the Nationalist Northern Army were quickly redeployed to fight in the Madrid sector. In the first days of the offensive, two Italian fighter squadrons stationed near Toledo and a Spanish Ju 52 bomber unit stationed at Talavera were put under the Legion Condor's command, and then by 9 July, additional Italian bomber units were also placed under Legion Condor command as the Legion Condor deployed the rest of its forces as quickly as possible from the northern front to the Madrid sector.

It was a sign of the maturity that the Legion Condor had achieved after a year of combat that the planning and logistics of moving the entire force – and taking command of the Spanish and Italian air units as well – was done very quickly and smoothly. In the first days of the battle, more than 200 German, Spanish Nationalist, and Italian aircraft would be united under the Legion Condor's operational command to fight in the Brunete sector. In addition to moving the aircraft, the Legion Condor also deployed part of its flak battalion to the most threatened sector of the front.

The elite Navarrese 150th Division was quickly redeployed from the north of Spain thanks to hundreds of American trucks that had been bought on credit by the Nationalist government. America, along with France and Britain and other western nations, had banned the sale of arms to both belligerent sides in Spain, but had not banned regular commercial trade. The American auto manufacturers and oil companies were free to do business, and big American companies preferred to bet on Franco's government rather than the Communist-friendly Republic. During the war Ford, General Motors and Studebaker companies sold Franco 12,000 trucks and Standard Oil provided 3½ million tons of fuel – all on credit. For the Nationalists, vehicles and gasoline were far more useful than any arms America might have provided. The Nationalist motor vehicle fleet enabled Franco's army to quickly redeploy its elite divisions around Spain to react to any crisis at the front. In the first days of the offensive at Brunete the Nationalist 108th Division, following the Navarrese 150th Division, was also redeployed to the Brunete sector. The Nationalists built up a substantial counter-attack force to deliver a powerful blow against the Republic.

The Legion Condor that arrived at the battle of Brunete was a very different force from the one that had gone into combat just three months before in northern Spain. The bomber units were all being re-equipped with He 111 bombers and the Ju 52 bombers transferred to the Nationalist Air Force. Dornier Do 17s now constituted a flight of long-range aircraft for the Legion Condor's reconnaissance squadron. Seventeen Bf 109s had arrived in Spain, had been assembled, and now equipped a squadron of the Legion Condor's fighter group, with some aircraft in reserve. The Legion Condor still had its force of Heinkel He 51 close-support fighters, and the experience of the campaign in the Basque country had been important in developing the Legion Condor's close air support procedures.

For the first time, the Spanish Civil War saw large-scale aerial combat with modern aircraft contending for control of a small area. German fighters were flying up to three missions a day. Legion Condor bombers based at Avila and Salamanca were flying at least two sorties a day. Both sides had good airfields nearby so both could maintain a high sortie rate. Legion Condor logistics units performed very effectively.

During the battle of Brunete, the Spanish Republicans and Nationalists both conducted very aggressive campaigns. For the first days, it was the Republicans that had the advantage in numbers and initiative. They carried out several attacks on Nationalist airfields and also attacked Nationalist units on the front. The outnumbered Nationalists flew defence, and primarily targeted the logistics of the Republican forces. The towns just behind the Republican lines, and Brunete and Villanueva de la Cañada, which had become forward logistics points, were heavily bombed by the Legion, as the Legion fighters and bombers worked to delay the Republican forces.

Condor Legion flak batteries were some of the first units deployed to support the hard-pressed Nationalist front. The 20mm light flak gun performed well in the direct-fire mode in ground operations, with its 20mm shell effective against Republican vehicles and even the thin-skinned Republican tanks. (Author's collection)

During the battle of Brunete most Condor Legion bombers were based at Avila. (Author's collection)

In the first days the Legion Condor lost two He 70s to Republican anti-aircraft guns. Indeed, at least five Republican batteries were active on the Brunete front, and the He 51 fighter pilots recalled the intense anti-aircraft fire when they were flying against the front units of the Republicans. On 10 July, the Legion Condor lost a Bf 109 and its pilot, and the next day a Legion Bf 109, flown by Feldwebel Boddem, shot down a Republican I-15 flown by the American pilot Harold Dahl. He was subsequently captured and held by the Nationalists. On 16 July the main Legion Condor bomber base at Avila was attacked by Republican SB-2 fast bombers, but these attacks caused only moderate damage.

By 11 July, the Republican attack had ground to a halt, taking heavy losses while having gained only a moderate salient into the Nationalist front. The Legion Condor flak units, which had first arrived on the front lines on 9 July, can claim some credit for holding the line. A single German flak battery was credited with crippling a dozen Republican tanks.

For a week, heavy fighting continued back and forth. On 18 July the Nationalists began their first major counter-offensive, which struck the eastern flank of the Republican salient held by the XVIII Corps and pushed it back several kilometres in five days of heavy fighting. The tide had clearly turned in favour of the Nationalists. The Nationalists had general air superiority over the Brunete front, thanks to the Bf 109s. And the Nationalist offensive was supported by 60 batteries of artillery. More than 200 German, Spanish, and Italian aircraft, working in a coordinated fashion, pummelled the Republican front lines and the logistics and communications right behind the front. The Republican artillery was a priority target and during the counter-offensive Spanish and German Ju 52 bombers carried out night attacks on Republican airfields.

After a brief operational pause the second Nationalist counter-offensive began on 22 July. This attack was aimed at the Republican V Corps occupying Brunete and the southern flank of the salient. The climax of the battle came on 24–25 July. The Nationalist 13th Division took Brunete on the 24th, and prepared to attack the main Republican defence line 1km north of Brunete. The elite Republican 11th Division had dug successive deep trenches in a cemetery located on a hill, which dominated the surrounding terrain and was the main Republican strongpoint. In addition to trench lines the 11th Division had placed tanks and two artillery pieces on the hill. The Nationalist 13th Division attacked the position on the afternoon of the 25th, as the Condor Legion made a maximum effort with every available fighter and bomber to support the 13th Division. Condor Legion

Spanish soldiers carrying bombs for the Germans at Avila airbase, summer 1937. The Condor Legion logistics troops were able to store and supply large amounts of munitions and fuel during highly intense periods of combat such as the Brunete campaign. (Author's collection)

bombers pounded the Republican defences while flights of He 51s made successive low-level attacks to suppress the defenders' fire. The devastatingly effective air support enabled the Nationalists to break the Republican defence and advance a further 4km to Hill 662. This advance effectively ended the Brunete campaign.

The battle of Brunete saw the Republic take 25,000 casualties, with its best units decimated. Most of the armour of the Republican Army had been lost, destroyed, or disabled, and approximately half the fighter force of the Spanish Republic had been lost in battle. The International Brigades, the elite forces of the Republic, had lost a third of their numbers as battle casualties, and were suffering from extremely low morale. The Republican Air Force lost approximately 100 aircraft in the Brunete campaign, while the Nationalist air forces lost 23 aircraft. The Nationalists lost far fewer tanks and guns than the Republic. The final verdict shows that this was in fact one of the truly decisive battles of the war. In several ways, it spelled the beginning of the end for the Republican cause.

The Brunete campaign had been the best chance for the Republic to gain a decisive victory in the war, and they failed. The Republican advance was too cautious, and it allowed the Nationalists, who reacted very quickly and very effectively, to pour in reinforcements and build an effective defensive line. The Spanish Republic underestimated the Nationalist forces and failed to plan effectively for communications and logistics, which were carried out poorly in the Republican planning and advance. On the other hand, the Nationalist ground forces had shown that they could react very quickly and very effectively. The general liaison and coordination of the ground forces and the air forces (despite some friendly-fire incidents) were highly effective, and the general doctrine of the Legion Condor of flying escort for the bombers and then flying fighter sweeps to clear the sky proved effective. Here, the first large-scale combat between the new Bf 109s and the Republic's I-16 and I-15 fighters showed the decisive superiority of the Bf 109 in fighter combat. The Nationalists' ability to gain air superiority was key to their success. The German flak forces operating in the direct-fire mode proved to be especially effective. Finally, the Brunete campaign also showed that the Germans were capable of operating as a coalition command element for a major air campaign. The Legion Condor's signals battalion worked very effectively, and the liaison system of German officers assigned to Spanish headquarters worked well.

Return to the north, August 1937

After the intense battle of Brunete, there was a need to repair and overhaul the Condor Legion's aircraft before returning to northern Spain and concluding the campaign that had been interrupted in early July. The Legion Condor was still receiving new aircraft and its personnel needed a period of further instruction on the Bf 109 fighters and He 111 bombers. As the battle of Brunete wound down, the signal companies of the Legion Condor returned north to the Asturias region, the last Republican enclave in the north. At the end of July, the fighter group of the Legion Condor had been reorganized into three squadrons: two squadrons with 18 He 51s between them, and one squadron with nine Bf 109s. The goal of the next stage of the Nationalist defensive would be Santander, where the Republicans had two squadrons of I-16s and two squadrons of I-15 fighters. There was a mix of Soviet and Spanish pilots at Santander, and the Republicans possessed various other Potez and Nieuport fighters and bombers, as well as an array of transport aircraft. For the coming campaign, the Legion Condor would have both quantitative and qualitative superiority.

The Legion Condor opened the new offensive in the north on 7 August when it struck Republican airfields near Santander and destroyed ten Republican fighters. The Legion Condor bomber force had returned to the north, and the bomber wing was now composed

of 18 Ju 52 bombers and 14 He 111s. The reconnaissance squadron of the Legion Condor possessed six He 70s and three Do 17s. For the last stage of the Northern Offensive, the Legion Condor had several Spanish Nationalist air units placed under their command. However, the Italians would be fighting in their own sector on the front in the north, and their aircraft would be supporting that sector. The Legion Condor, with its Spanish squadrons attached, had approximately 115 aircraft. The major ground offensive towards Santander began on 14 August. By now, both the Spanish and the Germans had perfected some of their close air support techniques. A new experiment was tried in the north that turned out to be very successful. The He 51 could be equipped with a 170-litre drop tank, but instead of using it to extend range, the Legion Condor attached two 10kg fragmentation bombs to the petrol-filled tank and dropped it as an early form of napalm, and this weapon proved exceptionally effective in the ground attack.

In this photo we see three squadrons of Condor Legion aircraft. Leon was developed by the Condor Legion as a major logistics and repair depot for the campaigns in the north in 1937. The Condor Legion mechanics based here managed to keep the operational readiness rate of the Condor Legion aircraft high. (Author's collection)

The Nationalist ground offensive, with very effective close air support and air superiority over the entire front, progressed very rapidly. On 16 August, Reinosa, which contained Spain's largest small-arms factory, was captured by the Nationalists, and the factory now began to produce weapons for Franco's forces. The Legion Condor carried out more strikes on Republican airfields and further decimated the Republican aircraft. By 22 August, the Nationalists had claimed more than 30 Republican aircraft shot down, and on 25 August Santander, one of the major Republican strongholds in northern Spain, fell to the Nationalists. After Santander, there remained a clearing operation through September and into October, driving the last Republican forces out of Asturias. On 21 October, the campaign in Asturias was declared closed, and the last surviving Republican forces had been evacuated through the port city of Gijon. At the airfield at Gijon, the Republican Air Force left behind four I-15 and four I-16 fighter planes in good condition, and these were quickly crated up and transported to Germany and studied intensively by the Luftwaffe staff.

The Condor Legion opened the campaign in Asturias in 1937 with a series of devastating attacks against the Republican airfields in the Asturias. Having destroyed most of the Republican aircraft on the ground, the Condor Legion saw little air opposition in the Asturias campaign that cleared northern Spain of its last Republican enclave. (Author's collection)

Teruel: holding the line in Aragon, December 1937– February 1938

Before the end of 1937, the Legion Condor would prove again that it could quickly redeploy to another front while in the midst of major combat operations. While the Nationalists were preparing for an offensive in the Madrid area, ten Republican divisions carried out a surprise attack against the Nationalist front in Aragon, at the town of Teruel, on 15 December 1937. With a Republican force of 80 bombers, 100 fighters and reconnaissance aircraft as well as numerous Soviet-supplied flak guns, the Republicans were able to gain local air superiority for the first days of the campaign. The Legion Condor, now under the command of General Helmuth Volkmann (General Sperrle had returned to Germany on 30 October), directed the redeployment of the Legion Condor to the mountainous Teruel front in the midst of the Spanish winter. By this time, the weather was a far more dangerous enemy than the Republican Air Force. Flying in mountainous terrain with heavy blizzards and icing, the Legion Condor had to learn to conduct cold-weather operations. The maintenance officers and NCOs improvised numerous methods to keep the German aircraft flying, such as putting special warming hoods around the engines, and heating engine oil before flying. The Nationalists soon won air superiority along the Teruel front and, by late December, the Nationalist ground forces were ready for a major ground attack.

The effectiveness of the Legion Condor in close-support operations was again demonstrated at Teruel. On 29 December, the Nationalist counter-attack was led by the Legion Condor and the Nationalist Air Force, which was improving rapidly in its capabilities. The German and Nationalist air forces conducted a saturation bombing of the Republican front lines and paved the way for Nationalist infantry to break through. Once the Republican lines were broken, the Legion Condor switched its attention from the front lines to interdicting Republican reinforcements. The Nationalist counter-attack made limited gains until blizzards grounded all air operations and enabled the Republican forces to hold the line. Both the air and the ground fighting around Teruel became an attrition battle during January and

early February 1938, until the Nationalist counter-offensive finally regained the city on 17 February. The fighting at Teruel witnessed the baptism of fire for the newly arrived Ju 87 Stukas, which carried out dive-bombing attacks in support of the Nationalist Army. By the end of the Teruel campaign in February 1938, the Republican fighter force had been largely destroyed, most falling prey to the Legion Condor's Bf 109 fighters.

The 88mm flak gun could be used as a conventional artillery piece as well as serving as an anti-aircraft gun. With a maximum range of 22.5km the 88mm was very useful in supporting the ground battle. Because of the Nationalist shortage of modern artillery, the Condor Legion heavy flak batteries were used extensively to support the ground battles. (Author's collection)

Levante offensive: the drive to the Mediterranean, March–April 1938

The Teruel campaign had left the Republican forces in poor shape. At the beginning of the campaign, the Republic's army and air force had near-parity with the forces of the Nationalists. By the end of the Teruel campaign, the Republicans had suffered heavy losses and, particularly seriously, heavy losses in tanks, aircraft, artillery, and materiél. Basic supplies of ammunition were short, and the Republican Army on the Aragon front was completely exhausted. Although new supplies of aircraft and equipment were arriving in early spring 1938 from the USSR, it would take time to incorporate the Soviet weapons into the Republican Army, and to replace the lost artillery.

The Nationalists chose this moment for a major offensive, with four corps along the Aragon front, with the aim of driving an 80-mile wedge through the middle of the Spanish Republic to the Mediterranean. The aim of the drive was to separate Catalonia from the rest of Republican Spain and its capital at Valencia. The Nationalist forces had not lost much equipment in the Teruel campaign, and in the air especially the Nationalists had a strong superiority. The overall plan called for the Legion Condor to be committed to the support of the Navarre Corps and the Aragon Corps. The Morocco Corps would be supported by the Nationalist Air Force and the Italian Corps, and one Nationalist division would be supported by the Italian Expeditionary Force. The battle opened on 22 March with air units striking hard at the Republican airfields, and especially the Republican rail and road network. On

7 April the effort switched, with Legion Condor bombers now conducting major attacks on the Cartagena and Almira ports to interdict supplies coming from the USSR. By this point, the close air support provided by the Legion Condor and the Nationalist Air Force was rated as very effective and the shattered and worn-out Republican forces on the Aragon front began to break. The Nationalists made rapid advances in early April that resembled the Blitzkrieg operations that would be seen in France in 1940. On 14 April the Nationalist forces reached the Mediterranean at Vinaroz, and cut the Spanish Republic in half.

This was one of the signal victories of the war, and it offered the Nationalists a tremendous opportunity. At this point, General Volkmann of the Legion Condor advised Franco that the resistance on the Catalonian part of the front was very weak, and that there was an excellent opportunity for Spanish Nationalist forces to turn north and quickly clear all Catalonia of Republican forces. Franco, however, disregarded Volkmann's advice. In one of Franco's few major strategic mistakes he ordered the Nationalist forces and the Legion Condor to turn their attention to the south and begin an offensive towards Valencia to seize the Republican capital.

Despite frictions the Nationalist coalition proved effective. In several campaigns, particularly in Aragon and

Volkmann did not get along with Franco as well as Sperrle did, but he proved to be a very competent commander of the Condor Legion in the tough campaigns from Teruel to the Ebro. (Author's collection)

the April battles of 1938, the three ground and air forces cooperated well. While reporting on the success of the Nationalist interdiction campaign, General Volkmann remarked that despite every effort, a system of full command authority for the three coalition air forces through the Spanish Air Force chief was not to be achieved. However, it was not actually necessary for success. At the operational level of war, senior commanders generally agreed to cooperate and jointly coordinate the battle action. The coordination problems often came from the political leaders, not the military. For example., during the Teruel campaign Mussolini ordered the Italian commander in Spain to withhold Italian air support until Italian ground forces were allowed into the battle.

The Ebro offensive: the last great battle, July–November 1938

On 24–25 July 1938, the Republican Army launched a surprise offensive from Catalonia south across the Ebro river. The Republicans had amassed an impressive force of 100,000

Two examples of the first pre-production models of the Ju 87 (Ju 87A) arrived in Spain at the end of 1937. The Ju 87 saw its debut in February 1938 during the Teruel offensive. Only a few Ju 87As were built and these were underpowered with a 640hp engine. Normally the A model carried only one 250kg bomb. While more of an experimental model, the Ju 87A proved its ability to hit small targets with great accuracy. (Author's collection)

men and were well supported by tanks and artillery. Aircraft were another matter. Because of the Nationalist offensive against Valencia, all the best Republican air units had been committed there and the commander of the Republican Northern Army in Catalonia had only 36 fighters and a handful of bombers and support aircraft to aid the offensive. As the campaign progressed the Republican Air Commander, General Cisneros, sent fighter groups to reinforce the north, but the initial attack was made with little air support. This would prove to be a fatal flaw in the offensive plan.

The assault across the Ebro river was initially successful and drove in part of the Nationalist defensive line. The Legion Condor at this time was carrying out air operations against the southern half of Republican Spain, but as soon as it was clear that a major offensive was under

Ju 87As strike the road junction at Ocala del Obispo

The first Ju 87 Stuka dive bombers were deployed to Spain in late 1936 and initially used to support the Nationalist forces at Teruel in February 1938. The three Ju 87s in Spain became 5.Staffel K/88, serving basically as test models. The A-model of the Ju 87, of which only a handful were built, were slow and underpowered, with their Jumo 210 engine providing only 640hp. To carry its maximum bombload of one 500kg bomb the Ju 87A had to fly without the observer/machine gunner. However, these first Ju 87s proved their worth in being able to hit targets with pinpoint accuracy. The Luftwaffe's dive bomber squadrons in Germany rotated personnel through Spain to gain experience with the new type.

On March 22 1938, the Nationalist Northern Army began its offensive in Aragon to overrun the Republican Army and break through to the Mediterranean, dividing Republican Spain in two. As the offensive began the Condor Legion carried out intensive attacks against the Republican airfields and the rail and road network in Aragon in support of two Nationalist army corps.

On 25 March a flight of Stukas from K/88 attacked the key highway junction at Ocala del Obispo, diving from 9,000ft to score a direct hit on the crossroads with a 500kg bomb. While it was an impressive feat of aerial marksmanship, the dry ground enabled the Republican Army to simply drive its columns around the huge crater made by the Stukas.

In late 1938 five Ju 87Bs arrived in Spain and were used extensively in the final battles of the war, especially in attacking rail lines and Republican ports. The Ju 87B had a 950hp Jumo 211 engine, which made it 60km/h faster than the A model and allowed it to carry 1,000kg of bombs.

OPPOSITE THE BATTLE OF EBRO

way, the Germans began to redeploy their force to meet the new threat. The Legion Condor again showed its flexibility for, within two days of the start of the offensive, the Luftwaffe began a massive interdiction campaign against the Republican lines of communication, which were especially vulnerable because they relied on supply by boat and bridges across the Ebro river. The main bridges and ferry points across the Ebro came under intensive air attack by the Legion Condor throughout the campaign. K/88 dropped 250 tons of bombs on the bridge at Flix; 671 tons on the Mora de Ebro bridges; at Ginestar 545 tons; and 39 tons at the ferry landing at Asco. This does not include the tonnage dropped by the Legion Condor's Stukas or the Nationalist and Italian bombers.

If the Republican Army was initially weak in aircraft it fielded a strong anti-aircraft force, and the bridges and ferry crossings on the Ebro, obvious targets for air strikes, were especially well-defended. Legion Condor battle reports mention the heavy and effective use of flak by the Republicans. In the Ebro campaign the Republican Army deployed six batteries of heavy flak, four batteries of 40mm flak, 16 batteries of 20mm flak and 12 lorries with multiple machine gun mounts.

Note the open four-aircraft formation and dramatic difference from the German tactical formations of 1936. Along with superior tactics developed by Werner Mölders, the high-performance Bf 109 was able to inflict heavy casualties on the Republican Air Force and ensure air superiority for the Nationalist coalition. (Author's collection)

As with so many battles of the Spanish Civil War, the Republic's army gained an initial advantage and then bogged down. The campaign soon became a war of attrition, including in the air war, as the Republican threw their best engineers into keeping the bridges and roads in repair and restoring logistics lines as quickly as the German and Nationalist air forces could damage them.

On the first day of the battle, General Yagüe conferred with General Volkmann and explained the crisis; Volkmann responded immediately, sending Legion Condor bombers and fighters to strike at the Ebro crossings and to search out any Republican columns. The Legion Condor's fighters and bombers flew several sorties a day in the first week in an attempt to blunt the Republican advance, as the Nationalists scrambled to send reinforcements to

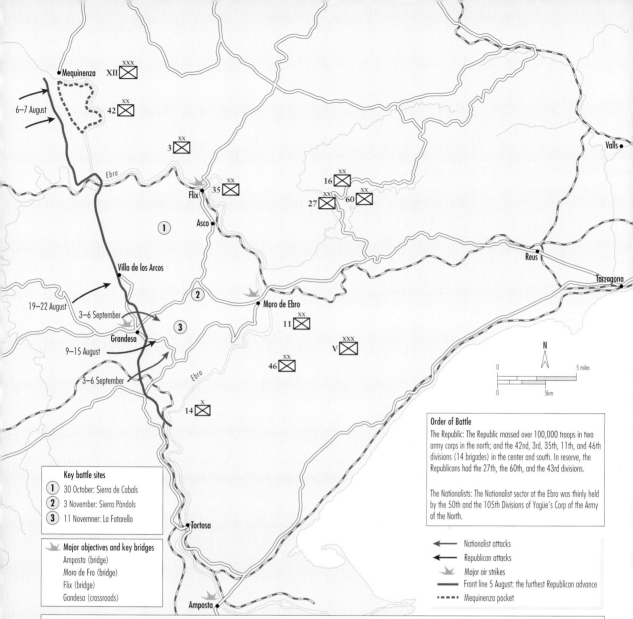

Mequinenza XII xxx

6–7 August

42 xx

3 xx

Flix 35 xx

16 xx

27 xx 60 xx

Asco

Villa de los Arcos

19–22 August

3–6 September

Grandesa

9–15 August

3–6 September

Moro de Ebro

11 xx

V xxx

46 xx

14 x

Valls

Reus

Tarragona

Ebro

N

0 ___ 5 miles
0 ___ 5km

Order of Battle

The Republic: The Republic massed over 100,000 troops in two army corps in the north; and the 42nd, 3rd, 35th, 11th, and 46th divisions (14 brigades) in the center and south. In reserve, the Republicans had the 27th, the 60th, and the 43rd divisions.

The Nationalists: The Nationalist sector at the Ebro was thinly held by the 50th and the 105th Divisions of Yagüe's Corp of the Army of the North.

Key battle sites

1 30 October: Sierra de Cabals
2 3 November: Sierra Pàndols
3 11 Novemner: La Fatarello

Major objectives and key bridges

Amposta (bridge)
Moro de Fro (bridge)
Flix (bridge)
Gandesa (crossroads)

⟵ Nationalist attacks
⟵ Republican attacks
⚑ Major air strikes
— Front line 5 August: the furthest Republican advance
····· Mequinenza pocket

Tortosa

Amposta

Events

The evening of 24/25 July, the Republicans launched their surprise attack at several points across the Ebro. The Republicans crossed at Punta Quemada, with the 42nd Division, as a diversionary attack in the north. The Republican 35th Division crossed the Ebro north of Asco. The Republican V Corps crossed the Ebro south of Mora de Ebro/Ginestar with three brigades, and further south, with another brigade north of Xerta. A small crossing was made at Amposta, the southernmost part of the breakthrough sector.

The Republican XV and V Corps drive on 25 July towards Gandesa as their main objective. On the first day, there is a dramatic advance, and the Republicans take the high ground at La Fatarella, and advance almost to Gandesa, taking the Sierra de Pàndols and Sierra de Cavalls, just to the east overlooking Gandesa.

On 26 July, the 900-man garrison at Mora de Ebro surrenders. The Republicans have set up bridges at Flix, and captured bridges at Mora de Ebro and Amposta.

In the night of 25/26 July, Nationalists reinforce and send units from the 13th, 82nd, and 4th divisions en route, along with tanks and a group of 77mm guns, to hold the line at Gandesa.

Between 26 July and 2 August, the Republican XV Army Corps attempts to break the Nationalist lines at Villa Alba de los Arcos [Cat: Vilalba dels Arcs] and Quattro Caminos [Cuatro Caminos alt.], which is an important crossroads. In a week of heavy fighting, the Republicans advance to the outskirts of Villa alba de los Arcos but fail to take the town. In front of Gandesa, the Nationalists built a defensive line and manage to hold the line. By 5 August, the Republicans have reached their furthest points of advance and now, in the face of increasing Nationalist reinforcements and firepower, go on the defensive.

The first major Nationalist counter-offensive is the destruction of the Fayón Mequinensa pocket on 6–7 August. The pocket of the Republican 42nd Division is attacked by reinforced units of the 82nd Division, including extra artillery and tanks. In a two-day battle, the Republican 42nd Division enclave is eliminated as the Republicans retreat across the Ebro.

On 9–15 August in the Sierra de Pàndols [Serra de Pàndols] the Nationalists counter-attack, supported by successive waves of Nationalist and German aircraft. The 11th and 35th Republican Divisions hold on.

On 19–22 August, the Nationalists attack at Villa alba de los Arcos [Vilalba dels Arcs] with the 74th and 82nd divisions and 200 guns in support, but they make small gains for heavy losses.

By late August the Nationalists are reorganizing and have brought 350 artillery pieces into the sector. There is a tactical offensive at Sierra del Lavall de la Torre on 3–6 September, and the 1st Navarese Division and 13th Nationalist Division, supported by the Condor Legion – and especially, Condor Legion flak – inflict heavy casualties on the Republican 27th Division. The Republicans reinforce and hold their position on 10–11 September to prevent a Nationalist advance to the Sierra de Cavalls [Cat: Serra de Cavalls].

On 2–4 October the 1st and 4th Nationalist Divisions reach the peaks of Sierra del Lavall de la Torre, and suffer heavy casualties, the 1st Navarrese Division losing 4,612 men.

The final offensive during the Ebro Campaign lasts from 30 October to 16 November. Seven Nationalist divisions strike at the northern and southern wings of the Republican enclave. There is a long attrition battle at the Sierra de Pàndols [Serra de Pàndols], but eventually the Republicans are forced out. At the Sierra de Cavalls [Cat: Serra de Cavalls], the Nationalists have success when the four Nationalist divisions, supported by massive artillery barrage and continuous bombing attacks by the Condor Legion and Nationalist Air Force, wreck the defending Republican 130th Brigade with air attacks. On 16 November the last of the Republican forces evacuate back across the Ebro River.

The Battle of the Ebro was an attrition battle on the ground and in the air. Republicans and Nationalists altogether lost approximately 40,000 casualties. The Republicans lost a considerable amount of equipment that was irreplaceable, including 35 tanks.

The Condor Legion, Nationalist Air Force, and Italian Air Force all expended maximum effort to interdict Republican movement. (Author's collection)

the Ebro. Three days into the Republican attack, General Volkmann reported to Berlin that: 'Due to heavy air attacks by our whole force the temporary defensive positions on the Ebro can be held against strong Red attacks.'

The Legion Condor had air superiority over the Ebro front from the start of the offensive. In early August the Republican Air Force sent a group of fighters to their Northern Army, and more reinforcements would follow now that the Nationalists had stopped their drive on Valencia and concentrated all efforts to containing the Republican offensive. Still, the Republicans required that a large part of their air force be retained to defend Madrid and Valencia while air reinforcements were cautiously dribbled into Catalonia. This meant that the Republican air operations at the Ebro were almost completely defensive in nature as the ten fighter squadrons detailed to support the offensive were vastly outnumbered by the combined forces of the Germans, Nationalists and Italians. The Legion Condor fighter group introduced new tactics over the Ebro that made the disparity between the Nationalist and Republican air forces even greater. Instead of flying in close formations based on flights of three, the Germans now operated in pairs 300m to 500m apart. Each wingman looked out for the other and the wide separation was just close enough for pilots flying the fast Bf 109 to support each other if needed, and far enough apart to allow a large part of the sky to be observed. The pair of fighters was called a *Rotte* and two pairs would be called a *Schwarm*. *Schwarms* could reinforce and support each other, taking different altitudes and engaging an enemy from different directions. The Legion Condor fighters, now flying the much-improved and more heavily armed Bf 190C and -D models, now completely outclassed the Republic's best fighter, the I-16. During the intense air battles over the Ebro front during late July and August 1938, the Legion Condor fighters alone shot down 29 Republican aircraft.

While the Legion Condor fighters were decimating the Republican fighter force, the German bombers and Stukas conducted an intensive interdiction campaign against Republican bridges, logistics lines, reserve units and artillery batteries. By this time, the Legion Condor had received eight early-model Ju 87 dive bombers and six Henschel Hs 123 ground-attack aircraft. The Ju 87 dive bomber was used extensively by the Legion Condor in its interdiction campaign along the Ebro. The Stukas proved to be more accurate against point targets than the conventional bombers and the Legion Condor reported to Berlin that they were pleased with the Stuka's performance. The Ju 87s became a favourite weapon of the Legion Condor and were often ordered to fly between two and four sorties per day.

Before the war in Spain, it was believed that the dive bombers could expect very high attrition rates from ground fire. Yet in Spain, even though the Republicans had covered their front with a strong force of Russian 20mm and 45mm anti-aircraft guns, the attrition rate of the Stukas and other close-support aircraft was much lower than had been expected by the Luftwaffe staff. The Legion Condor reckoned that their rapid redeployment to the Ebro front and their ability to conduct an extensive interdiction campaign had played a central role in slowing and eventually halting the Republican offensive by the end of July.

By August 1938 the Legion Condor had turned its attention to a close air support campaign to blast Republican front lines, artillery positions, and troop reserves in support

The Luftwaffe sent six Ju 87B Stukas to Spain in autumn 1938. With a 950hp engine this model carried a heavier bombload and more armament and was 60mph faster than the early A-model. This is the variant that won fame in the 1939–40 *Blitzkrieg* campaigns and became a workhorse for Condor Legion operations. They were used to strike precise targets such as rail junctions, Republican airfields, Republican headquarters and depots. In late 1938 they took part in strikes against shipping in Republican ports. The Stukas proved effective in the anti-shipping role and were credited with sinking eight Republican ships. (Author's collection)

of the Nationalist counter-attack. For the next three months the Legion Condor supported a series of set-piece attacks, taking back the lost territory bit by bit. In these battles the Legion Condor's flak unit, employing both heavy and light batteries, found itself playing a key part of the battle. By the start of their final offensive in October the Nationalists could mass 350 artillery pieces to support attacks. Due to the crisis in European politics in the summer of 1938 the Luftwaffe was slow to send new pilots to replace the ones rotating home. General Volkmann ordered an acceleration of the training programme for Nationalist aircrews and Spanish pilots and crewmen were incorporated into the Legion Condor's bomber wing. The German crewmen reported that the Spanish airmen

He 111s bomb the bridge at Moro de Ebro, 14 August 1938

After the dramatic advances of the Republican Army across the Ebro in late July the campaign turned into a bloody stalemate. As the Republican Army depended on sending supplies and reinforcements across five pontoon bridges and ferry sites, these became major targets for the Condor Legion's bombers. The Republicans defended the bridge and ferry sites fiercely, surrounding them with heavy and light flak batteries, and deploying three groups of I-16 fighters to defend their forces in the Ebro salient.

On the afternoon of 14 August, nine He 111s of 1.Staffel K/88, under the command of Captain Heyse, attacked the bridge site with 250kg and 50kg bombs. Coming from the southeast at 12,000ft the bombers were escorted by the Bf 109C and -Ds of 2.Staffel J/88, commanded by Captain Walter Grabmann. The escort fighters flew above the bombers in the *Schwarm* or 'finger-four' formation. As the bombers approached the target they were met by heavy flak fire and 15 Republican I-16 fighters approaching from the west.

II.J/88 was outnumbered, but their Bf 109s were far superior to the Republican fighters. In addition, the Germans had the advantage of excellent training, experienced leadership and superior tactics. Republican commanders, while making a valiant attempt to reinforce the Ebro sector and improve their air force, noted that many of their new pilots (some of whom had just returned from training in Russia) were not adequately trained. The German fighters quickly broke up the Republican fighter attack and the Heinkel bombers made a successful bomb run against the bridge approaches. In this attack no Condor Legion aircraft was lost, although one bomber of I.K/88 was heavily damaged by flak.

An entire ridge line erupts in fire and smoke from a heavy bomber strike. Massed attacks had not only physical effects but also psychological effects upon the enemy. (Author's collection)

progressed very quickly. The final weeks of the battle, from 30 October to 16 November, saw a series of massive artillery bombardments combined with heavy bomber strikes that simply destroyed whole Republican brigades.

The Ebro campaign had been the most successful Legion Condor operation so far. The Legion had maintained a high sortie rate despite the shortage of aircrew. Converting the Spanish aircrews onto new aircraft such as the He 111 was proceeding faster than expected. In 113 days of intense battle – the longest and bloodiest campaign of the war – the Legion Condor had lost ten aircraft (to combat and accidents) and had seen 14 badly damaged. Only five aircrew had been killed and six captured. The Legion Condor claimed 100 Republican aircraft during the campaign – fully one-third of all Republican losses. Finally, the three air forces of the Nationalist coalition worked together very effectively. Careful coordination of air and ground units in a massive application of firepower had been the only means by which the Republican Army had been pushed out of the excellent defensive terrain of the Ebro hills.

The final campaign

The Ebro campaign ended on 16 November 1938 when the Republican forces were finally driven back across the Ebro river, and the front line resumed the positions held in July. The Ebro Campaign was a disaster for the Republic. On the ground, both sides had taken heavy losses, with Republican forces losing more men than the Nationalists. In the air battle, the Republicans lost more than 300 aircraft. The constantly growing and improving Nationalist air force accounted for more than one third of these losses, and the fighter units of the Legion Condor shot down a third of the Republican aircraft, with Mölders' 3.Staffel accounting for 42 of the Legion Condor's aerial victories.

In November the Legion Condor prepared itself for what would clearly be the final campaign, which would first aim to occupy all of Catalonia to the French border. The Legion Condor spent time reequipping its forces, and by December 1939 the Legion had 37 Bf 109B, -C, and -D fighters, approximately 40 He 111 bombers, fourJu 87 Stukas, five Do 17 reconnaissance aircraft, fiveHe 45 short-range reconnaissance aircraft, and eight He 59 seaplanes. This does not include a number of transport and liaison aircraft used by the Legion. The end of November also saw another change of command. In mid-November, *Generalmajor* Hellmuth Volkmann, who had done a competent job in the year that he had commanded the Legion, but certainly not won friends among the Spanish or Italians, returned to Germany to the army, where he was given a divisional command. The new commander, who was well known to everyone, was Wolfram von Richthofen, now a *Generalmajor*. He arrived on 30 November with his chief of staff *Oberstleutnant* Hans Seidemann. With the battle of the Ebro over, the Legion Condor concentrated the major part of its force at Lerida Airfield in Aragon.

In December the Nationalists began their advance towards Barcelona, supported by strong air forces of the Legion Condor, the Nationalist Air Force, and the Italian Air Force. With the Republican Air Force decimated in the Ebro Campaign, there was a slackening of Republican air resistance, although early in the campaign the Republicans did carry out some attacks against Nationalist airfields. At this point in the war, Spanish pilots were being trained on the Bf 109 and the Nationalists were equipping two of their own squadrons with Bf 109s transferred from the Germans, as well as He 112 fighters. The Legion Condor was now receiving the E-model of the Bf 109 and in early 1939, carried out the process of turning over the early B- and C-models to the Nationalists. At this point, the Nationalist fighter force included an array of German and Italian aircraft, including a number of the now-obsolete He 45s and He 51s. The Nationalist bomber force included some of the old Ju 52 bombers, but also two modern Ju 86s from Germany, as well as 14 Do 17s and two Henschel Hs 123 dive-bombers. At the end of December 1939, as the Nationalist advance moved into Catalonia, the Nationalist Air Force alone had more than 200 fighter planes, opposed by the Republic's 140 I-15 and I-16 fighters. The Soviet resupply of aircraft was tapering off as it became clear to the USSR that the Spanish Republic was a lost cause. The Republic's aircraft factory at Alicante built only 16 I-16 fighters, out of an anticipated contract of 100. However, the factory at Reus was able to build one I-15 fighter per day. During the war, as the Soviets had trained a large number of Spanish Republican pilots, there was also no shortage of pilots.

In the first advances into Catalonia, one of the Legion Condor's most successful contributions was its flak units, which performed extremely well in supporting the Nationalist ground attacks. The Legion Condor's air effort turned to heavy attacks upon the Port of Barcelona, as well as attacks on Republican airfields and forward forces as well as the rail network. On 7 January 1939, under orders to relieve the pressure in Catalonia, the Republican Army in the southern part of the Republic's territory launched a major attack towards Seville and pushed more than 30km into the Nationalist lines in the first week of its offensive. However, as the Legion Condor considered plans to relocate to the south, the Nationalist local air and ground forces managed to slow the Republican offensive, so no change of effort became necessary for the Legion Condor. Von Richthofen, at this time, recommended that the Legion Condor be returned to Germany as the war was effectively won and the Nationalist Air Force had shown that it could handle large-scale operations. The German high command turned down von Richthofen's request as 'it would send a wrong message' in the increasingly tense European scene.

On 12 January, the Legion Condor struck two of the main Republican airfields, destroying 13 aircraft on the ground. Despite

Throughout the war the German and Italian air forces made the strategic bombing of the Republican ports a top priority. By 1938 the constant attacks made it hard for the Russians to maintain the flow of war materials to the Republic. When the Nationalists occupied Barcelona in 1939 they found the port littered with dozens of sunken and wrecked ships. (Author's collection)

The Hs126 served very effectively as the Luftwaffe's standard short-range reconnaissance aircraft during World War II. It could easily operate from rough, forward airfields. (Author's collection)

poor weather in January, the Nationalist offensive sped up, with the light flak continuing to do excellent service. By late January, the forward Republican airfields had been overrun, and Republican forces were in full retreat.

Barcelona fell on 26 January, and with the Republican resistance in the north collapsing, the Legion Condor primarily carried out harassment and interdiction strikes on the retreating

Von Richthofen returned to Spain in November 1938 as a *Generalmajor* and commander of the Condor Legion. At this point Nationalist air superiority was overwhelming and the Condor Legion concluded the campaign with support to the Nationalist Army advance sweeping through Catalonia and with numerous strategic attacks against Republican transport and shipping. (Author's collection)

Here von Richthofen can be seen behind Franco. (Author's collection)

Republicans, attacking the rail stations. The main enemy of the Legion Condor at this point was Catalonia's winter weather, which caused aircraft losses on 5 February that included a Heinkel bomber. On 10 February, Nationalist forces reached the French border, and the campaign for Catalonia was over. In January and February 1939, the Legion Condor, in its final major campaign, shot down 47 Republican aircraft and destroyed another 31 on the ground. Several dozen Republican aircraft were captured. At the beginning of March, negotiations began for the surrender of the Republic's last enclave in Spain. The Legion Condor relocated closer to Madrid and carried out a number of attacks on forward Republican positions and Republican shipping. Legion Condor records indicate regular fighter sweeps over Madrid and central Spain, but with no Republican contact. On 25 March, delegates from the Republican government arrived in Burgos to negotiate the surrender. The Legion Condor flew its last mission on 27 March, attacking Republican Army lines around Madrid. On 28 March, Madrid surrendered, and the war was over.

ASSESSMENT

Effects of the Spanish Civil War on the Luftwaffe and Wehrmacht

The Luftwaffe's experience in the Spanish Civil War had an enormous impact upon Luftwaffe doctrine, tactics, and technology. From 1936 to 1939 over 19,000 Luftwaffe personnel served in Spain. On their return they spread throughout the force, which meant that when the Luftwaffe went to war in 1939 it had far more combat experience in modern warfare than any of its opponents. By the end of the Spanish Civil War, many senior Luftwaffe officers, including future field marshals Sperrle and von Richthofen, and future generals Drum, Plocher and Seidemann, had all gained recent command experience in a major war. Adolf Galland, later a Luftwaffe general and commander of the Reich's fighter defences, saw his first combat as a ground-attack pilot in Spain.

In Spain, the Luftwaffe had had the opportunity to conduct virtually every type of air campaign. The Spanish war featured strategic bombing, interdiction campaigns, naval anti-shipping campaigns, close air support and air superiority campaigns. The Luftwaffe had initially fought the war under conditions of a static front similar to those of World War I and, later in the war, under conditions of modern manoeuvre warfare with German aircraft flying in support of rapidly moving motorized formations. The combat record of the Legion Condor was impressive. The Luftwaffe had shot down 327 Spanish Republican aircraft. The Legion's flak battalion had proven its worth by shooting down an additional 59 Republican aircraft. Against this toll of 386 Republican aircraft the Legion Condor had lost only 72 aircraft in combat. The Luftwaffe seaplane squadron claimed a total of

Condor Legion troops leaving Spain at Vigo, May 1939. (Author's collection)

52 Republican ships destroyed and many other ships damaged. The Stuka detachment of the Legion Condor claimed eight enemy ships.

Total German casualties in Spain came to 298 dead. Of these, only 131 were killed in combat. Another 167 German personnel died in accidents or of disease. A further 139 were wounded in action and 439 injured due to other causes. Given the long period of combat and the high sortie rates of the aircraft, the high command in Berlin was surprised at the low losses suffered by the Legion Condor, which were far lower than had been estimated at the start of the conflict.

The success of the Luftwaffe close air support operations in Spain directly influenced the plans for the Polish campaign of 1939. The Luftwaffe consolidated more than half of the rapidly growing Stuka force into a 'close battle division' and placed it under the command of Wolfram von Richthofen. In a few months' time, its mission would be to replicate upon the Polish Army the effect that close air support operations had demonstrated in Spain.

One of the primary lessons of Spain was the importance of aerial navigation and night flying. Over the course of the war, the Luftwaffe lost more pilots and aircraft to operational accidents than it did to the Republican Air Force: 72 planes in combat, but 160 aircraft in operational accidents. In most cases, the accidents had occurred at night or in poor weather. German pilots trained to fly in daylight conditions were prone to fly their aircraft into Spanish mountainsides at night. These problems provoked some immediate changes in the Luftwaffe training programme. When General Sperrle returned to Germany in autumn 1937 and took over the Luftwaffe forces that would become Luftflotte 3, he immediately told his new command that bad-weather flying had not been pushed energetically enough. His first order was to require every unit in his command to conduct winter exercises and practise bad-weather operations and night flying. Thanks to the experience in Spain, the Luftwaffe became much better trained in fundamental navigation and flying skills. By the start of World War II it was the only air force in Europe that was even moderately competent at night flying and bad-weather navigation.

Operational lessons

The Legion Condor validated the effectiveness of the Luftwaffe's doctrine. The operational air war concept that combined ground and air efforts into a single campaign plan worked

The finger-four formation. The loose formation developed by Captain Werner Mölders proved far superior to the complicated fighter tactics in use since World War I. The World War I tactics emphasized very tight formations because fighter unit leaders relied on hand signals to communicate with their pilots. Effective voice radios installed in the advanced fighters of the late 1930s allowed fighter commanders to control their units in far superior wide and loose formations. (Author's collection)

He 51 fighters in standard combat formation above the river Rhine, 1936. The tight flights of three aircraft flying very close together (30m separation) dates back to World War I. Such close formations made sense in a pre-radio era when flight commanders communicated by hand signals. (Author's collection)

very well under all kinds of conditions. The Germans had learned that the problem was in the details. The Legion Condor now understood that army and air commanders needed to co-locate and their staffs needed to plan together. Modern warfare required a very robust communications and liaison system down to low levels. It took some months for the Germans and the Nationalist Army to become truly effective partners. Modern joint operations required extensive practice and training to work.

The Spanish Civil War had also highlighted the importance of air force logistics and support services. The extensive support infrastructure of the Legion Condor had allowed the force to rapidly move and open up new airfields when battle emergencies required the rapid redeployment of air units. The Legion Condor signallers could rapidly establish effective communications in new locations and link the air units to the headquarters. The fully motorized Legion Condor could move its support units quickly across Spain and keep the air units supplied with fuel and munitions.

The Legion Condor flak had certainly proved its worth. It had not only done a good job defending the Legion's airfields, but both light and heavy flak guns had proven entirely effective in supporting the ground war. Thanks to the lessons of Spain, the Wehrmacht High Command ordered an increase in flak guns for both the army and the Luftwaffe and using flak guns against ground targets became a standard practice.

Tactical lessons: Werner Mölders and the new fighter tactics

The Luftwaffe also learned many tactical lessons in Spain, but the most important one was a revolutionary change in fighter combat that would eventually change the way

Bf 109D squadron pilots getting their mission briefing. After the end of the Ebro campaign, the Condor Legion had a free hand in pursuing the remnants of the Republican Army. (Author's collection)

One of the key lessons to come out of Spain was the importance of good command and control (C2) systems, and close communication between the troops on the ground and supporting air units. The Germans took the C2 lessons of Spain and established them throughout the Luftwaffe. In the 1940 campaign, the superior German C2 and good communications between the air force and the ground army were far superior to those of the British and French forces and gave the Wehrmacht a decisive advantage. (Author's collection)

all air forces fought. One of the most important single figures of the Spanish Civil War was not a high-ranking officer, but rather a fighter pilot who arrived as a first lieutenant and replacement fighter-squadron commander. Yet this young officer, in a very short period, would play a central role in revolutionizing fighter tactics. Werner Mölders was born in 1913 in Westphalia. His father, a reserve officer, was killed in the battles of 1915, and he was raised by his mother's family in central Germany. He graduated from one of the top high schools of Germany in 1931, and with his Abitur (university entrance certificate) he applied to join the army as an officer aspirant. He was appointed to the 2nd Prussian Infantry Regiment and he went through the very thorough and intensive three-year officer education programme. In March 1934, Mölders was commissioned as a lieutenant and assigned to the new Luftwaffe. Mölders entered flight training and graduated at the top of his class. He then proceeded to the special six-month fighter-pilot course, and again graduated at the top in June 1935. In 1936, he was promoted to first lieutenant. Mölders took over command of a training squadron and served under group commander, Major Theo Osterkamp, who would also become one of the key figures in the Luftwaffe fighter force. In March 1937, Mölders was given command of Jagdgeschwader 334, and proved himself to be an exceptional commander as well as instructor.

Mölders volunteered to go to Spain, arriving in March 1938. He was assigned to take over Adolf Galland's fighter squadron, which was still equipped with the He 51 but in the process of transitioning to the Bf 109. In May 1938, after a short transition period, Mölders took over as squadron commander. Mölders was soon involved in the very tough fighting around Aragon and over the Ebro. He scored his first victory over an I-15 on 15 July 1938. Between July and 3 November 1938, Mölders would rack up 14 confirmed aerial victories, which made him the top German ace of the Spanish Civil War. His victories included two I-15s, 12 I-16s, and one SB-2 bomber. As Mölders led his squadron into the Aragon and Ebro battles, he began work on developing a revolutionary new tactical system for the fighters. The system used by all the major air forces up to that time had scarcely changed from World War I, in which squadrons of 9–12 aircraft would fly a very tight formation, usually based on the 'V' or flight of three aircraft. The tight aircraft formations, inherited from World War I combat, came from a period in which fighter aircraft did not have radios and needed to use hand signals; to observe these signals, pilots had to be sufficiently close to their flight and squadron leaders. Now that aircraft were more than twice as fast as the World War I biplanes, and equipped with radios, a Great War tactical system made no sense. Mölders developed a system based on pairs, in which one pair of wingmen, called a *Rotte*, would look out for each other, one usually forward and the other slightly above and behind. The *Rotte* could be enlarged with another *Rotte*, to make a loose formation of four aircraft called a *Schwarm*. This four-aircraft *Schwarm* replaced the three-aircraft flight, and was also called the 'finger-four formation' because it looked like the fingers of a hand, with two fingers, the second slightly ahead, and then a pair of fingers, the second aircraft again slightly leading.

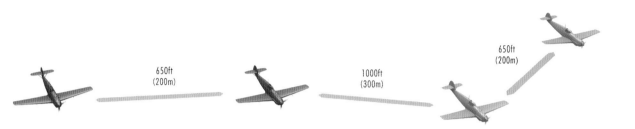

650ft
(200m)

1000ft
(300m)

650ft
(200m)

ABOVE THE 'FINGER FOUR', OR *ROTTE* AND *SCHWARM* TACTICAL FIGHTER FORMATIONS

From 1916 to 1938, all air forces based their fighter tactics on flights of three flying in very close formation (30m apart). Squadrons flew with three to four flights of three aircraft in complex squadron formations. It took time to organize the squadron formations, and rapid changes of direction or formation were difficult, with a high risk of collision due to the close formations.

Captain Werner Mölders' new fighter tactics developed for the Legion Condor and Nationalist Air Force were made possible by the new technology of aircraft voice radios. The radios enabled aircraft to fly with wide separations of 200–300m while flight and squadron commanders still could command their fighters. The new tactics were based on pairs of fighters and combinations of pairs. A pair of fighters (the *Rotte*) was the basic unit, with the first aircraft flying in front with the second flying slightly to the rear and often higher than his wingman. The lead aircraft looked to the front while the second aircraft covered his partner, looking to the rear and flank. When joined by another pair the four aircraft became a *Schwarm* (flight), with the four aircraft spread across more than half a mile of sky with the four aircraft (two flight leads slightly forward, two wingmen hanging slightly back) looking like the four fingers of an extended hand. Further *Schwarms* could be added on at different altitudes to create large fighter formations.

The 'finger-four' was simple, very effective in offence and defence, and allowed for room to manoeuvre. The new tactics also allowed a fighter squadron to cover much more of the sky, which allowed the German and Nationalist fighters to spot their opponents earlier and then move to gain height and position advantage.

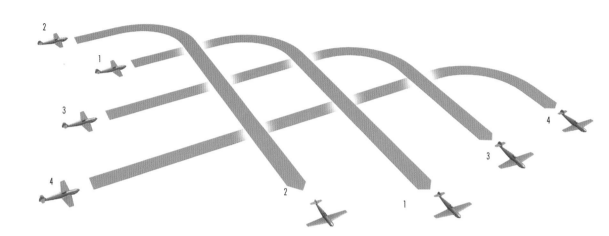

ABOVE 'SCHWARM TURN' OR CROSSOVER TURN

From World War I until the 1938 air battles in Spain, getting a fighter formation to turn 90 degrees was a complicated manoeuvre with a high risk of collision if not carried out properly. The standard three-aircraft flight formation used in all major air forces was awkward to manoeuvre. After creating the basic 'finger four' formation, Captain Mölders created a new manoeuvring system. In order to change direction 90 degrees, the left-hand pair made a sharp turn and became the right-hand pair. The right-hand pair flew straight a few seconds longer and then turned sharply and became the left-hand pair. The whole manoeuvre could be accomplished in seconds. The wide separation of 200–300m between the aircraft minimized any collision danger.

The 'finger four' formation and crossover turn gave German fighters a huge tactical advantage over their opponents – not just in Spain in 1938, but over France and the Low Countries in 1940.

Now fighter squadron tactics would be based on pairs and small groups. Instead of a 30m spread between aircraft, as in the old tactics, aircraft could now fly 300–500m apart, since radio contact provided them with effective communications. By spreading out and pairing the fighters, a more extensive area of the sky could be patrolled and observed, and the danger of midair collisions was largely eliminated. Given the speed of the Bf 109, any *Schwarm* engaging in combat could be quickly joined by other *Schwarms*. Mölders trained his fighter pilots in the new tactics. He also developed a new way to turn a flight in combat. Previously, a tight change of direction for a flight or squadron was an exceptionally dangerous manoeuvre because of the very narrow separation between aircraft. Now, with a wider separation, Mölders invented the crossover turn, in which aircraft would simply pivot 90 degrees and switch positions.

The new fighter tactics proved so successful against the Republican pilots that when Mölders completed his tour, he was brought back to the Luftwaffe staff and given a special mission in the Fighter Inspectorate: to develop and train the Fighter Command in this new tactical system. Mölders only served eight months in Spain, from March to December 1938, when he turned over his squadron to Hubertus von Bonin and received his promotion to captain. However, those eight months in Spain assured Mölders' reputation as a superb leader and fighter tactician. Mölders was quickly promoted up to command groups and wings. He was a major and group commander in the 1940 campaign in France and by 1941 had achieved the rank of colonel, or *Oberst*, and commanded a fighter wing in Russia. That year he was appointed Inspector of the Luftwaffe Fighters, but served only a brief time in that position as he was killed in an accident in November 1941. He was the first fighter pilot in the world to gain more than 100 confirmed aerial victories. The impact of his new tactics was so dramatic that eventually, all the combatant air forces of World War II would adopt the system of pairs, the finger-four formation, and the crossover turn that had been invented by Mölders.

Mölders emerged as the Condor Legion's top fighter pilot (14 victories), but his most important accomplishment was creating the revolutionary new fighter tactics that included the crossover turn and finger-four formation. The new fighter tactics gave the Luftwaffe a significant edge over their opponents in 1940. Mölders became a fighter wing commander and Inspector of Luftwaffe Fighter Forces in 1941. He was killed in an air accident late in 1941. (Photo by Keystone-France/Gamma-Keystone via Getty Images)

BIBLIOGRAPHY

Abendroth, Hans-Henning, 'Guernica: Ein fragwürdiges Symbol', in *Militärgeschichtliche Mitteilungen* 1/87, pp. 111-126

Azner, Manuel (1958), *Historia Militar de la Guerra de Espana, Vol I.*, Editoria Nacional, Madrid

Beevor, Antony (2006). *The Battle for Spain: The Spanish Civil War, 1936–1939* Penguin Books. London

Cortada, James (1982), *Historical Dictionary of the Spanish Civil War*, Greenwood Press, Westport, CT

Corum, James (1997), *The Luftwaffe: Creating the Operational Air War, 1918–1940*, University Press of Kansas, Lawrence, KS

Drum, Karl (1957), *The German Air Force in the Spanish Civil War*, USAF Historical Studies 150, Air Force Historical Support Division, Washington, DC

Estado Mayor del Ejercito (1963), *Historia Militar de la Guerra de Espana, Vol III* (Altimira S. A., Madrid

Franks, Norman (1986), *Aircraft Versus Aircraft*, Crescent Books, New York, NY

Hallion, Richard (1989), *Strike From the Sky: The History of Battlefield Air Attack, 1911–1945*, Smithsonian Institution Press, Washington, DC

Henry, Chris (1999), *The Ebro 1938: Death Knell of the Republic*, [Campaign 60], Osprey Publishing, Oxford

Howson, Gerald (1998), *Arms for Spain: The Untold Story of the Spanish Civil War*, Murray, New York, NY

Jackson, Gabriel (1967), *The Spanish Republic and the Civil War 1931–39*, Princeton University Press, Princeton, NJ

Jackson, Gabriel (1974), *A Concise History of the Spanish Civil War*, Thames and Hudson, London

Landis, Arthur (1968), *The Abraham Lincoln Brigade*, Citadel Press, New York, NY

Larios, José, (1965) *Combat Over Spain*, Neville Spearman, London

Legion Condor (1939), *Deutsche Kämpfen in Spanien*, Wilhelm Limpert Verlag, Berlin

Obermaier, Ernst and Werner Held (1986), *Jagdflieger Oberst Werner Moelders*, Motorbuch Verlag, Stuttgart

Payne, Stanley (1987), *The Franco Regime: 1936–1975*, University of Wisconsin Press, Madison, WI

Payne, Stanley, (2012), *The Spanish Civil War*, Cambridge University Press, Cambridge

Proctor, Raymond (1983), *Hitler's Luftwaffe and the Spanish Civil War*, Greenwood Press, Westport, CT

Richardson, R. (1993), 'The Development of Air Power Concepts and Air Combat Techniques in the Spanish Civil War', in *Air Power History* (Spring 1993)

Ries, Karl and Hans Ring, (1992), *The Legion Condor: A History of the Luftwaffe in the Spanish Civil War, 1936–1939*, Schiffer Military History, West Chester, PA

Thomas, Gordon and Max Witts (1975), *Guernica: The Crucible of World War II*, Stein & Day, New York

Thomas, Hugh (1987), *The Spanish Civil War*, Penguin Books, London

Westwell, Ian (2004), *Legion Condor: The Wehrmacht's Training Ground*, Ian Allan Publishing, Hersham, UK

Whealey, Robert (1989), *Hitler and Spain: The Nazi Role in the Spanish Civil War, 1936–1939*, University Press of Kentucky, Lexington

Wyden, Peter (1983) *The Passionate War: The Narrative History of the Spanish Civil War*, Simon and Schuster, New York, NY, pp 357–358

INDEX